Introductory Level

T0288575

SECOND EDITION

STEP FORWARD

STANDARDS-BASED LANGUAGE LEARNING
FOR WORK AND ACADEMIC READINESS

SERIES DIRECTOR
Jayme Adelson-Goldstein

Workbook

Vanessa Caceres

OXFORD
UNIVERSITY PRESS

OXFORD
UNIVERSITY PRESS

198 Madison Avenue
New York, NY 10016 USA

Great Clarendon Street, Oxford, OX2 6DP, United Kingdom

Oxford University Press is a department of the University of Oxford. It furthers the University's objective of excellence in research, scholarship, and education by publishing worldwide. Oxford is a registered trade mark of Oxford University Press in the UK and in certain other countries

First published in 2017
2022
10 9

ISBN: 978 0 19 449310 9 (Workbook Introductory Level)

Printed in China

This book is printed on paper from certified and well-managed sources

ACKNOWLEDGMENTS

Illustrations by: Argosy Publishing: 14, 30, 62. Shawn Banner: 73 Niki Barolini: 8, 10, 21, 23, 25, 28, 29, 35, 41, 42, 51, 56, 63, 64, 70, 76, 78. Barbara Bastian: 3, 77, 81, 84. Kenneth Batelman: 65, 72, 72, 72, 86, 87, 92, 93. John Batten: 2, 12, 17, 18, 39, 45, 62, 79. Richard Carbajal/illustrationonline.com: 21, 31, 44, 67. Laurie A. Conley: 24, 34, 50, 66 Bill Dickson/Contactjupiter.com: 13, 33. Jody Emery: 48, 69, 72, 75. Mark Hannon: 2, 32, 46, 59, 68, 82. Kev Hopgood: 5, 33, 34, 38, 48, 57, 61, 74, 75, 81. Rose Lowry: 4, 26, 52, 80. Mark Mones/AAReps.Inc.: 11, 20, 27, 32, 49, 55, 71. Pamorama.com: 6, 16, 51, 60, 74. Geo Parkin: 15, 37. Roger Penwill: 30 Linda Pierce: 4, 41, 53, 83, 89. Susan Spellman: 34, 40, 47, 55, 76. Simon Williams/illustrationweb.com.

The publishers would like to thank the following for their kind permission to reproduce photographs: Cover, Click Bestsellers/Shutterstock.com; pg. 24 Antonio Guillem/Shutterstock; pg. 36 Pakhnyushchy/Shutterstock, Pete Spiro/Shutterstock, Konstantin Labunskiy/Alamy Stock Photo, Zoonar GmbH/Alamy Stock Photo, elenovsky/Shutterstock, Melinda Fawver/Shutterstock, Patricia Hofmeester/Shutterstock, Pete Spiro/Shutterstock, Pakhnyushchy/Shutterstock, Pakhnyushchy/Shutterstock; pg. 58 Jaak Nilson/Getty Images; pg. 70 James R. Martin/Shutterstock, Paul Maguire/Shutterstock, Richard Goldberg/Shutterstock, Ashley Cooper/Getty Images; pg. 94 Amazingmikael/Shutterstock, Polkadot_Photo/Shutterstock, kupicoo/E+/Getty Images.

CONTENTS

UNIT 1 Nice to Meet You

LESSON 1 VOCABULARY

A **Match the words with the pictures.**

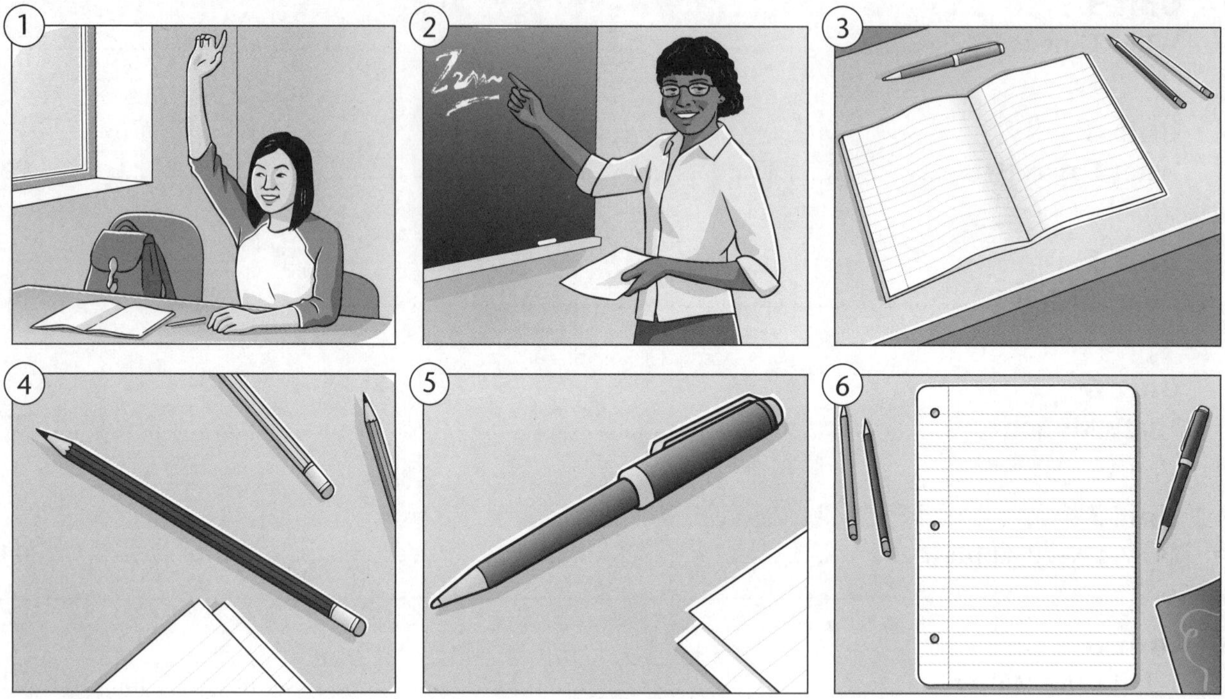

__1__ student	____ pen	____ paper
____ pencil	____ teacher	____ book

B **Complete the sentences. Use the words in the box.**

book ~~student~~ teacher pen paper

1. I'm a __student__.
2. Open the ____________.
3. Write on the ____________.
4. Write with the ____________.
5. He's a ____________.

A **Count the items. Write the number on the lines.**

1. ____4____ books
2. ________ pens
3. ________ pencils
4. ________ pictures

B **Write the numbers on the lines.**

1. 19 ____nineteen____
2. 7 ____________
3. 16 ____________
4. 5 ____________
5. 12 ____________
6. 11 ____________
7. 13 ____________
8. 8 ____________

LESSON 3 GRAMMAR

A Look at the pictures. Write the words. Use *he, she, it,* or *they*.

1. they

2. ______

3. ______

4. ______

5. ______

6. ______

B Complete the sentences. Circle *a* or *b*.

1. ____ is a man.
   a. She (b.) He
2. ____ are students.
   a. He b. We
3. ____ is a woman.
   a. She b. He
4. ____ are books.
   a. It b. They
5. ____ is a picture.
   a. It b. They

C Complete the sentences. Use *is* or *are*.

1. Mai ___is___ a student.
2. John __________ a teacher.
3. The teacher __________ a man.
4. You __________ a student.
5. It __________ a pencil.
6. They __________ books.
7. We __________ men.

D Match. Complete the sentences.

_c_	1. We	a. is a man.
____	2. He	b. are a woman.
____	3. I	c. are teachers.
____	4. It	d. am Kofi.
____	5. She	e. is a woman.
____	6. You	f. is a book

E Unscramble the sentences.

1. teacher / is / He / my
   He is my teacher.
2. women / They / are
   ____
3. a / clock / is / It
   ____
4. are / students / We
   ____
5. My / name / Rosa / is
   ____
6. man / a / I / am
   ____

A **Complete the conversation. Use the words in the box.**

is	you	meet	~~am~~

Jin: Hi, I ___am___ (1) Jin. What's your name?

Anna: My name ________ (2) Anna.

Jin: Nice to meet ________ (3).

Anna: Nice to ________ (4) you too.

B **Circle the words that start with *m*.**

A: Hello. I am (Mal.)

B: Excuse me?

A: Mal. M-A-L.

B: Hi. I am Mary.

C **Match the questions with the answers.**

__c__ 1. Hi, I am Lorena. What's your name?

____ 2. Excuse me?

____ 3. Nice to meet you.

a. Sal. S-A-L.

b. Nice to meet you too.

c. My name is Sal.

DO THE MATH Go to page 86.

A **Read the list.**

Milford Adult School
Teacher: Carla Boatman
Student: Leo Salas

School supplies

a binder
two pens
an English dictionary
a notebook
two pencils
an eraser

B **Look at A. Circle *a* or *b*.**

1.	a. paper	b. two pens
2.	a. a pencil	b. two pencils
3.	a. an eraser	b. a student ID
4.	a. two binders	b. an English dictionary
5.	a. a binder	b. a book
6.	a. two notebooks	b. a notebook
7.	a. Milford Adult School	b. Adams Adult School
8.	a. Carla Boatman is a student.	b. Carla Boatman is a teacher.
9.	a. Leo Salas is a student.	b. Leo Salas is a teacher.

A Circle the words in the puzzle. Use the words in the box.

~~pens~~	chair	they	students	she	nice
meet	book	eraser	table	binder	pencil

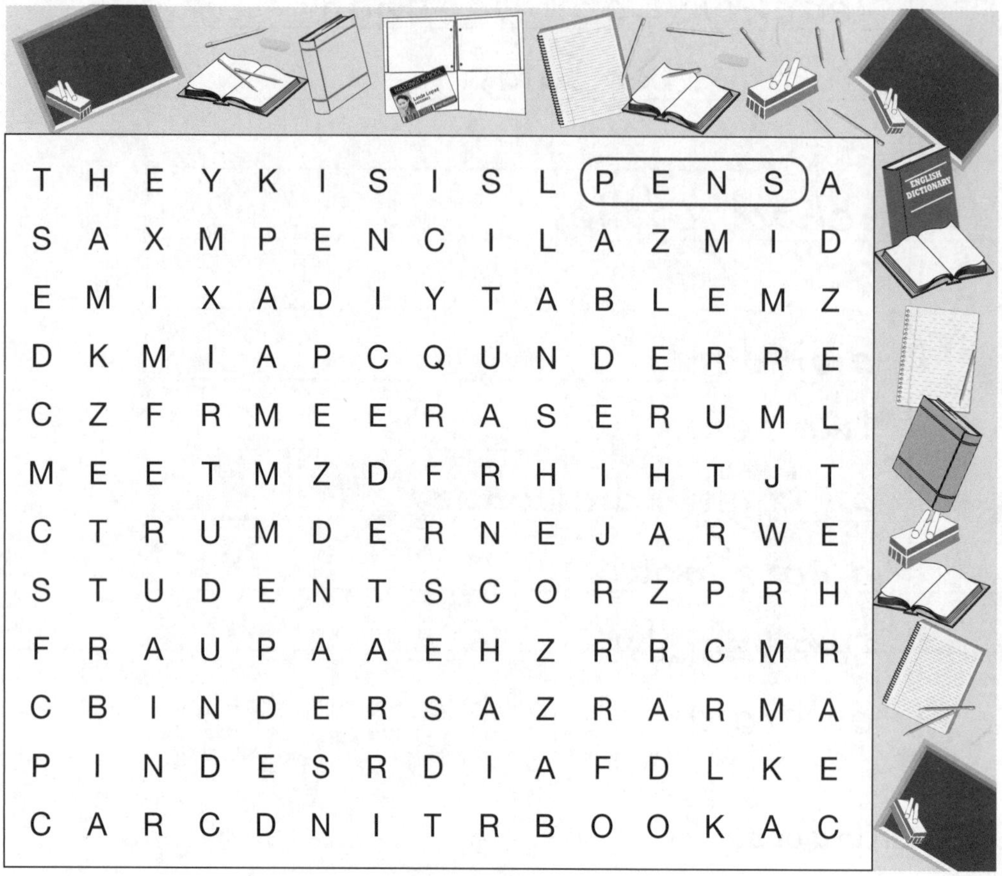

T	H	E	Y	K	I	S	I	S	L	P	E	N	S	A
S	A	X	M	P	E	N	C	I	L	A	Z	M	I	D
E	M	I	X	A	D	I	Y	T	A	B	L	E	M	Z
D	K	M	I	A	P	C	Q	U	N	D	E	R	R	E
C	Z	F	R	M	E	E	R	A	S	E	R	U	M	L
M	E	E	T	M	Z	D	F	R	H	I	H	T	J	T
C	T	R	U	M	D	E	R	N	E	J	A	R	W	E
S	T	U	D	E	N	T	S	C	O	R	Z	P	R	H
F	R	A	U	P	A	A	E	H	Z	R	R	C	M	R
C	B	I	N	D	E	R	S	A	Z	R	A	R	M	A
P	I	N	D	E	S	R	D	I	A	F	D	L	K	E
C	A	R	C	D	N	I	T	R	B	O	O	K	A	C

B Complete the words in each sentence with one letter. Use the letters in the box.

a	e	~~i~~	o	u

1. C__i__rcle number f__i__ve.
2. Nic____ to m____ ____t you.
3. My first n____me is Roxana.
4. They are my n____teb____ ____ks.
5. Yo____ are a st____dent.

UNIT 2

How Are You Feeling?

LESSON 1 VOCABULARY

A **Match the words with the pictures. Use the words in the box.**

~~fine~~ happy sad excited hungry tired thirsty sick

1. fine
2. ____________
3. ____________
4. ____________
5. ____________
6. ____________
7. ____________
8. ____________

B **Look at the chart. Circle *yes* or *no*.**

1. Jerry is tired. (yes) no
2. Joan is hungry. yes no
3. Corbin is happy. yes no
4. Kathy is sad. yes no

Name	Feeling
Jerry	tired
Joan	excited
Corbin	happy
Kathy	sick

A **Look at the form. Complete the sentences. Use the words in the box.**

~~Lian Wong~~	happy	Greenville, Texas	China

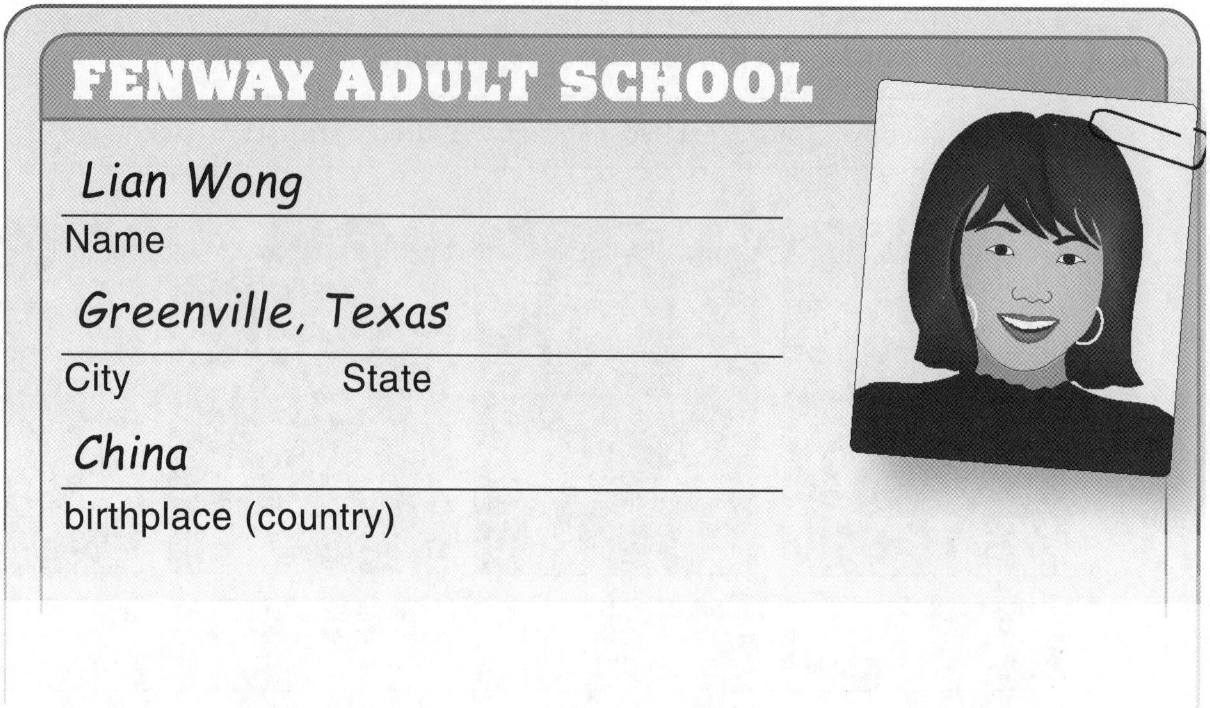
FENWAY ADULT SCHOOL

Lian Wong
Name

Greenville, Texas
City State

China
birthplace (country)

1. My name is Lian Wong.
2. I am from ______________________.
3. Now I am in ______________________, ______________________.
4. I am ______________________.

B **Look at the form in A. Circle *yes* or *no*.**

1. Lian is from China.	(yes)	no
2. The city is Texas.	yes	no
3. The state is Greenville.	yes	no
4. She is sad.	yes	no

A Complete the sentences. Circle *a* or *b*.

1. She ____ hungry.
   (a.) is not   b. are not
2. You ____ happy.
   a. is not   b. are not
3. The students ____ thirsty.
   a. is not   b. are not
4. Lam ____ sick.
   a. is not   b. are not
5. We ____ sad.
   a. is not   b. are not
6. Anita ____ tired.
   a. is not   b. are not

B Look at the pictures. Complete the sentences. Use *is, is not, are,* or *are not*.

1. She ___is not___ sick.
2. He ____________ hungry.
3. They ____________ happy.
4. Sal ____________ tired.
5. Inez ____________ tired.
6. They ____________ thirsty.

C Match. Complete the sentences.

_b_ 1. She   a. are not tired.
____ 2. I   b. is not hungry.
____ 3. We   c. am not sad.

D Complete the sentences. Use *am not, is not,* or *are not*.

1. The students ___are not___ sad.
2. I ____________ happy.
3. We ____________ hungry.
4. You ____________ excited.
5. Chris ____________ fine.
6. Marta ____________ thirsty.

E Write new sentences. Use contractions for the underlined words.

1. I am excited. ______I'm excited.______
2. She is from Haiti. ____________________
3. You are not thirsty. ____________________
4. I am from Dallas, Texas. ____________________
5. They are not hungry. ____________________
6. We are fine. ____________________

F Look at the picture. Write sentences. Use *He's* or *He's not* and the words in parentheses.

1. (happy) ______He's happy.______
2. (a teacher) ____________________
3. (in Riverside) ____________________

G Write sentences. Use contractions for the underlined words.

1. She / is / not / tired

   She's not tired.

2. I / am / happy

   ____

3. He / is / from / Colorado

   ____

4. We / are / not / hungry

   ____

5. It / is / not / my / book

   ____

6. They / are / sick

   ____

A Complete the conversation. Use the words in the box.

sorry	I'm	~~are~~	feeling

Petra: Hi, Ali. How __are__(1) you feeling?

Ali: I'm fine. How are you ________(2)?

Petra: ________(3) sick.

Ali: Oh, I'm ________(4).

B Match the questions with the answers.

__d__	1. How are you feeling?	a. I'm from Mexico.
____	2. What's your name?	b. He's from South Korea.
____	3. Where are you from?	c. My name is Zita.
____	4. How is she feeling?	d. I'm tired.
____	5. Where is he from?	e. She's fine.

DO THE MATH Go to page 86.

A Read the envelope.

Springfield Adult School
38 West Street
Springfield, GA 31329

Luis Salas
1242 Lee Street
Rincon, GA 31326

B Look at A. Circle *yes* or *no*.

1. The return address is 38 West Street, Springfield, GA 31329. (yes) no
2. The mailing address is 1242 Lee Street, Rincon, GA 31326. yes no
3. The school is in Springfield. yes no
4. Luis's address is 38 West Street. yes no
5. The school zip code is 31326. yes no
6. Luis's zip code is 31329. yes no

C Complete the sentences. Use words from the envelope in A.

1. The school is Springfield Adult School.
2. The school's city is ____________________.
3. The school's zip code is ____________________.
4. The student is ____________________.
5. The student's street is ____________________.
6. The mailing address is ____________________.

A Look at the pictures. Match the pictures to the sentences.

a

b

c

d

__a__ 1. Leila and Gerry are happy.

____ 2. Leila is tired.

____ 3. Now she is excited.

____ 4. She is sad.

B Complete the words in each sentence with one letter. Use the letters in the box.

a	e	~~i~~	o	u

1. Camille __i__s from Ha__i__t__i__.
2. Wh____r____ ar____ you from?
3. Ricardo is fr____m C____l____rad____.
4. Yo____ are h____ngry.
5. Wh____t's your n____me?

UNIT

3 What Time Is It?

LESSON 1 VOCABULARY

A Match the words with the pictures.

__f__ 1. It's midnight.

____ 2. It's 7:30.

____ 3. It's 3:00.

____ 4. It's 8:30.

____ 5. It's noon.

____ 6. It's 6:00.

B Look at the pictures in A. Complete the words.

1. m o __r__ __n__ i __n__ g
2. n ____ ____ n
3. a ____ t ____ ____ ____ ____ o n
4. e ____ ____ ____ i ____ g
5. n ____ ____ ____ ____
6. m ____ d ____ ____ ____ ____ ____

A **Look at the pictures. Complete the sentences. Use the words in the box.**

~~work~~	English class	home	clinic	store	library	school

1. I go to ____work____ at 7:30.
2. I go to the ______________ at 3:30.
3. I go to the ______________ at 4:30.
4. I go to the ______________ at 5:00.
5. I go to ______________ at 6:30.
6. I go to ______________ at 7:00.
7. I go ______________ at 9:00.

B **Complete the chart. Use the times in the box.**

~~8:00 a.m.~~	~~8:00 p.m.~~	7:30 p.m.	10:30 a.m.	10:15 p.m.	7:45 a.m.

Morning	Evening
8:00 a.m.	8:00 p.m.

LESSON 3 GRAMMAR

A Complete the questions. Use *Is* or *Are*.

1. ___Is___ she at work?
2. ________ you at the store?
3. ________ David at the library?
4. ________ they at the clinic?
5. ________ it 3:15?

B Match the pictures and the questions.

a

b

c

d

__c__ 1. Is she at home?

____ 2. Is he at the store?

____ 3. Are you at school?

____ 4. Are they at the library?

C Complete the questions and answers. Circle *a* or *b*.

1. Is it 2:00 ____
   (a.) ? b. .
2. She's at the clinic ____
   a. ? b. .
3. Is he at home ____
   a. ? b. .
4. Is it midnight ____
   a. ? b. .
5. They're in English class ____
   a. ? b. .
6. He's at work ____
   a. ? b. .

D Complete the conversations. Use *am, is,* or *are*.

1. **A:** Are they at work? **B:** Yes, they <u>are</u>.
2. **A:** Is Gary at home? **B:** Yes, he ________.
3. **A:** Is it 3:30? **B:** Yes, it ________.
4. **A:** Are you at the store? **B:** Yes, I ________.
5. **A:** Are we tired? **B:** Yes, we ________.
6. **A:** Is she at school? **B:** Yes, she ________.

E Write new sentences. Use contractions for the underlined words.

1. No, <u>they are</u> not. <u>No, they're not.</u>
2. No, <u>we are</u> not. ________________
3. No, <u>I am</u> not. ________________
4. No, <u>it is</u> not. ________________
5. No, <u>she is</u> not. ________________
6. No, <u>he is</u> not. ________________

F Read the answers. Then write *yes/no* questions. Use the words in parentheses.

1. (Emily / Georgia)

   A: <u>Is Emily from Georgia?</u>

   B: No, she's not.

2. (Susan / sick)

   A: ________________

   B: Yes, she is.

3. (the students / English class)

   A: ________________

   B: Yes, they are.

4. (you / library)

   A: ________________

   B: No, I'm not.

5. (it / 6:45)

   A: ________________

   B: No, it's not.

LESSON 4 EVERYDAY CONVERSATION

A Complete the conversation. Use the words and time in the box.

library	is	10:00	~~time~~

Pao: Excuse me. What ___time___ (1) is it?

Diego: It's ________ (2) .

Pao: Is the ________ (3) open?

Diego: Yes, it ________ (4) .

B Match the questions with the answers.

__d__	1. What's your name?	a. I'm from Colorado.
____	2. Are you a student?	b. It's 4:30.
____	3. Where are you from?	c. Yes, I am.
____	4. Is the school open?	d. My name is Pilar.
____	5. What time is it?	e. Yes, it is.

DO THE MATH Go to page 87.

LESSON 5 READING

A Read the train schedule.

Train Number	Helen	Fenway	River City	Maple
55	8:00 a.m.	8:20 a.m.	9:30 a.m.	11:00 a.m.
86	1:00 p.m.	1:20 p.m.	————	4:15 p.m.
10	3:30 p.m.	————	5:00 p.m.	6:30 p.m.
25	5:00 p.m.	5:20 p.m.	6:30 p.m.	8:00 p.m.

B Look at A. Circle *yes* or *no*.

1. Train 55 is at Fenway. Is it 8:20 a.m.? (yes) no
2. Train 25 is at Helen. Is it 6:30 p.m.? yes no
3. Train 86 is at Maple. Is it 4:15 p.m.? yes no
4. Train 10 is at River City. Is it 5:00 p.m.? yes no

C You are at Fenway. Look at the train schedule. Circle *a* or *b*.

1. How long is the trip to River City on Train 55?
   a. 1 hour and 10 minutes
   b. 2 hours and 10 minutes
2. How long is the trip to Maple on Train 25?
   a. 2 hours and 4 minutes
   b. 2 hours and 40 minutes

UNIT 3 ANOTHER LOOK

A **Complete the sentences. Use the words in the box.**

noon	minutes	midnight	~~home~~	train	time	morning	evening

Across

1. Is Mona at ____home____?
4. The ______________ is at Fenway at 1:20 p.m.
5. The store is open at ______________.
6. At 12 a.m., it is ______________.
8. The trip is 30 ______________.

Down

2. English class is a night class. It's in the ______________.
3. I go to work in the ______________.
7. What ______________ is it?

B **Write the words in the crossword puzzle.**

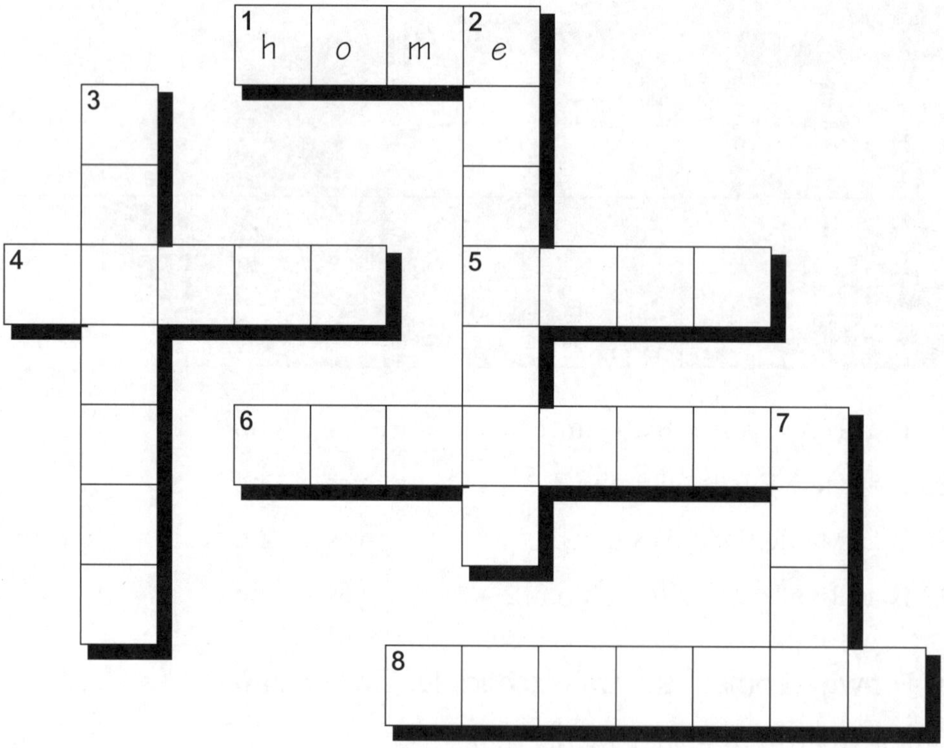

What Day Is It?

LESSON 1 VOCABULARY

A **Look at the picture. Write the missing letters.**

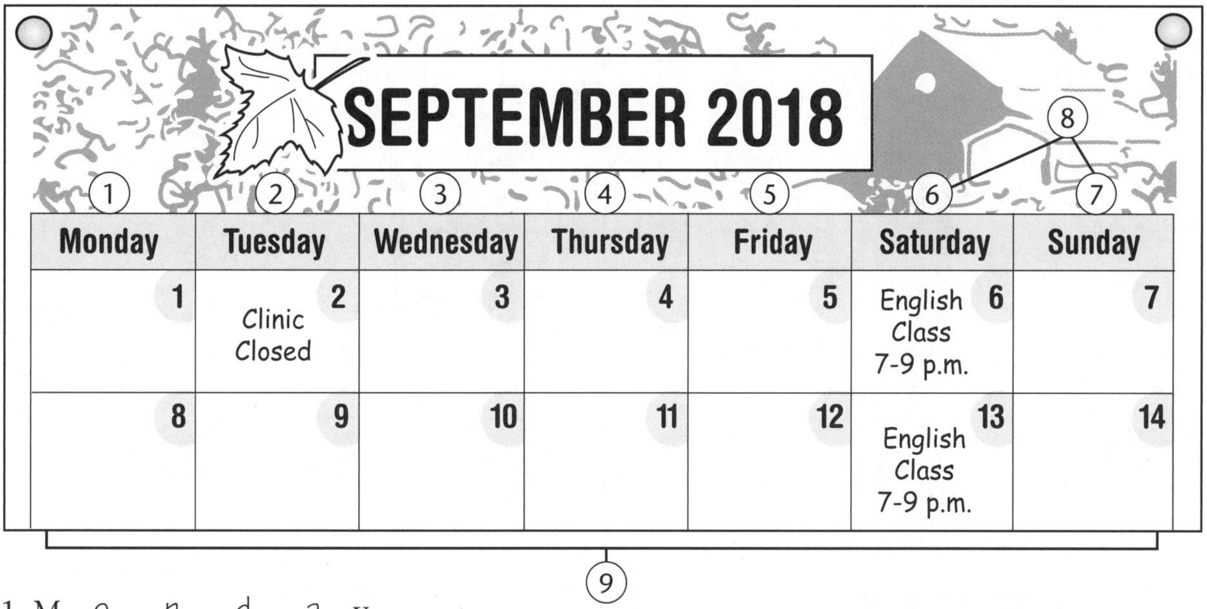

1. M _o_ _n_ _d_ _a_ y
2. T ____ ____ s ____ ____ y
3. W ____ ____ n ____ ____ ____ ____ ____
4. T ____ u ____ s ____ ____ ____
5. F ____ ____ d ____ ____
6. S ____ t ____ ____ ____ a ____
7. S ____ ____ d ____ y
8. w ____ ____ ____ e ____ ____
9. w ____ ____ ____

B **Look at the picture in A. Circle *yes* or *no*.**

1. Today is Tuesday. Tomorrow is Wednesday. (yes) no
2. The clinic is closed on Thursday. yes no
3. English class is on Monday and Wednesday. yes no
4. Today is Friday. Tomorrow is Saturday. yes no

A **Look at the picture. Complete the sentences. Use the words in the box.**

~~May~~	June	month	August	July

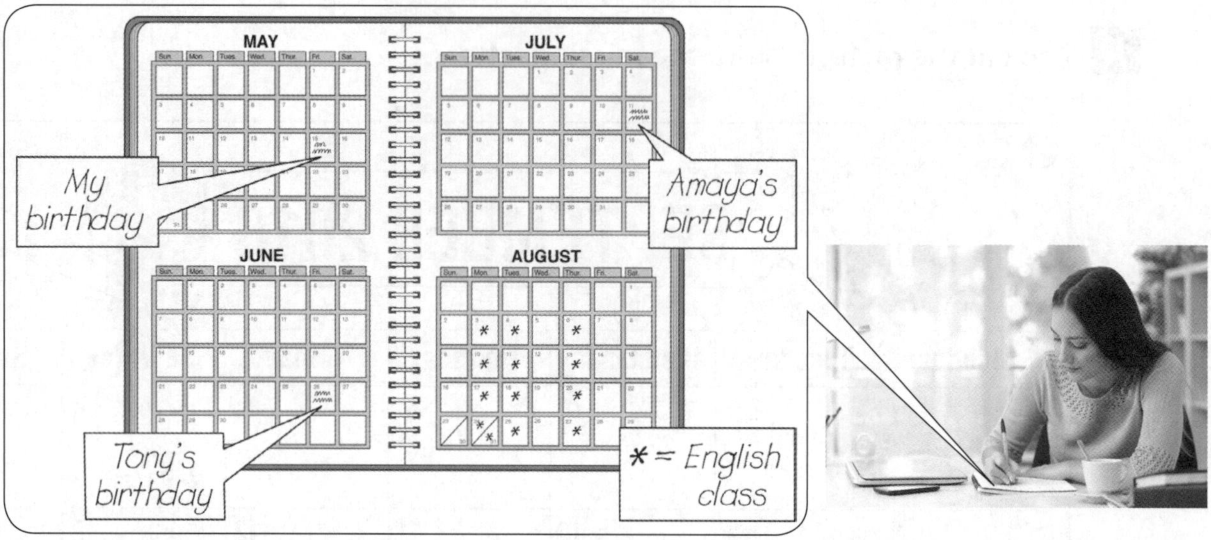

1. My birthday is in ______May______.
2. Tony's birthday is in ____________.
3. Amaya's birthday is in ____________.
4. It's July. Next ____________ is August.
5. English class is in ____________.

B **Complete the chart. Use the words in the box.**

~~Wednesday~~	~~February~~	Thursday	Sunday
March	Friday	December	October

Days of the week	Months
Wednesday	February

A **Complete the sentences. Circle *a* or *b*.**

1. The party is ____ Friday.

   (a.) on b. at

2. School is ____ Tuesdays and Thursdays.

   a. on b. at

3. English class is ____ 7:00.

   a. on b. at

4. The birthday party is ____ 8:00.

   a. on b. at

5. I go to work ____ 7 a.m.

   a. on b. at

6. I go to the library ____ Saturdays.

   a. on b. at

B **Look at the pictures. Write two sentences about each picture. Use *on* or *at* and the words and times in parentheses.**

1. (Wednesday)

   The class party is on Wednesday.

2. (3:00)

   ____

3. (Saturday)

   ____

4. (5:00)

   ____

C Complete the conversation. Use *What, Where,* or *When.*

1. **A:** Where is the party?
   B: It's at school.
2. **A:** ______ is the party?
   B: It's on Friday.
3. **A:** ______ time is the party?
   B: It's at noon.

D Match the questions with the answers.

d 1. When is the birthday party?
____ 2. When is English class?
____ 3. What time is English class?
____ 4. Is English class on Wednesdays?
____ 5. Where is the birthday party?
____ 6. Are you excited?

a. It's at 6:30.
b. It's on Mondays.
c. Yes, I am!
d. It's on Saturday.
e. Yes, it is.
f. It's at Atlanta Pizza.

E Unscramble the sentences.

1. party / 8:00 / class / The / at / is
   The class party is at 8:00.
2. class / My / Maple Adult School / is / at
   ______
3. The / birthday / Tuesday / party / on / is
   ______
4. house / at / my / party / is / The
   ______
5. Thursday / on / class / is / English
   ______
6. birthday / January / in / My / is
   ______

A **Complete the conversation. Use the words and time in the box.**

Bye Thursday nice 9:00 ~~What~~

Alfredo: What (1) time is it?

Deenah: It's ______ (2).

Alfredo: Thanks. Have a ______ (3) evening.

Deenah: Thanks. You too. See you ______ (4).

Alfredo: ______ (5).

B **Circle the words that start with *w*.**

A: Excuse me. (When) is the class party?

B: It's on Wednesday.

A: Thanks. Have a nice weekend.

B: You too. See you next week.

DO THE MATH Go to page 88.

A Read the class calendar.

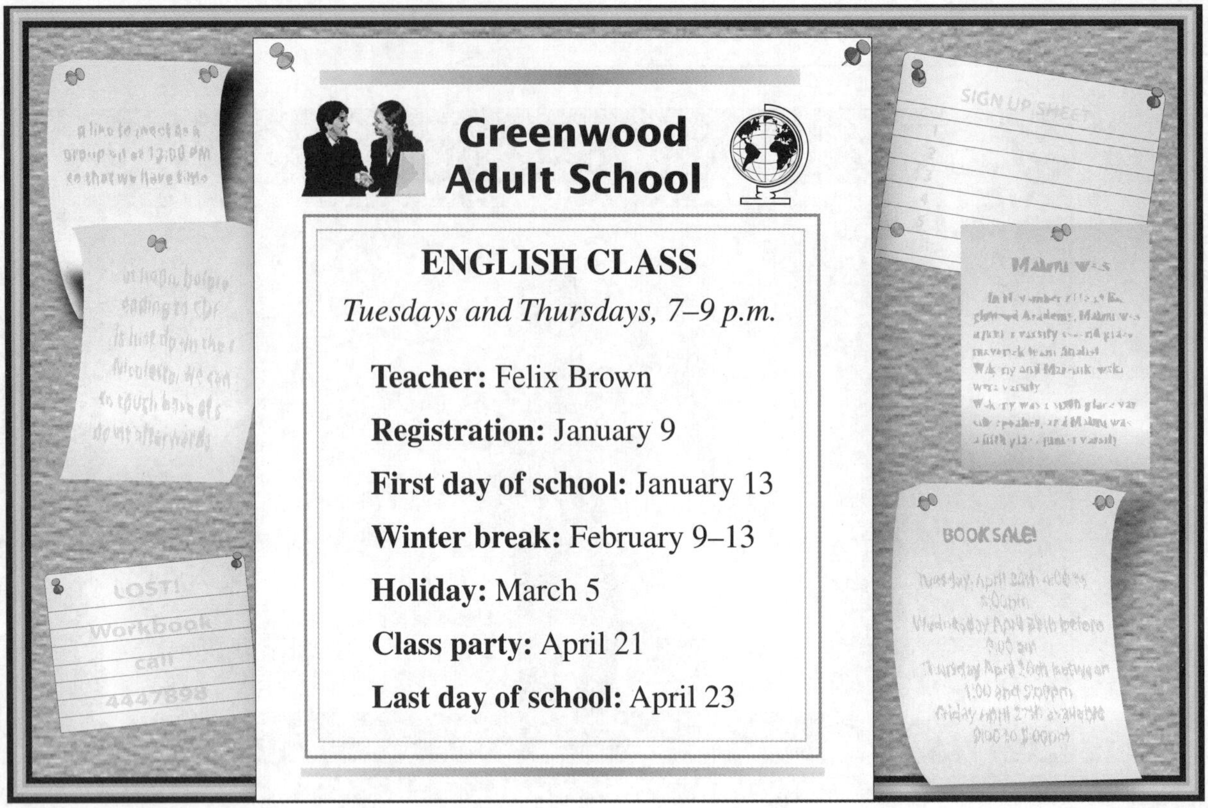

B Look at the class calendar in A. Complete the sentences.

1. Registration is ____January 9____.
2. Winter break is from February ________ to February ________.
3. ________________ is the class party.
4. The last day of school is ________________.
5. English class is on Tuesdays and ________________.

C Look at A. Circle *yes* or *no*.

1. The teacher is Felix Greenwood.	yes	(no)
2. English class is 7–9 p.m.	yes	no
3. The first day of school is January 14.	yes	no
4. The class party is in February.	yes	no
5. Registration is on Tuesdays and Thursdays.	yes	no
6. The holiday is on March 5.	yes	no

A Circle the words in the puzzle. Use the words in the box.

September	registration	weekend	~~month~~	second	where
Thanksgiving	October	goodbye	when	today	seventh

A	M	X	R	E	G	I	S	T	R	A	T	I	O	N
M	O	N	T	H	E	D	G	O	O	K	Z	N	B	P
W	C	R	L	S	C	L	T	M	A	B	R	A	X	Y
C	T	N	D	E	R	E	W	E	E	K	E	N	D	W
M	O	O	P	C	X	M	S	I	R	U	S	I	Y	S
S	B	A	T	O	D	A	Y	W	R	K	O	P	N	E
D	E	E	M	N	E	N	D	E	M	F	S	C	H	V
T	R	I	M	D	J	Y	L	U	A	B	O	O	L	E
Q	D	E	C	O	W	W	H	E	R	E	K	L	E	N
T	H	A	N	K	S	G	I	V	I	N	G	H	U	T
P	A	A	M	O	P	R	J	N	B	R	I	G	N	H
T	S	E	P	T	E	M	B	E	R	V	A	W	L	L
B	D	A	R	W	O	H	N	I	B	O	R	H	M	E
E	Z	O	D	S	X	G	O	O	D	B	Y	E	E	H
R	E	I	T	R	A	Y	D	R	O	G	P	N	N	O

B Complete the words in each sentence with one letter. Use the letters in the box.

a e ~~i~~ o u

1. Have a n__i__ce even__i__ng.
2. T____m____rr____w is M____nday.
3. S____ ____ you in S____pt____mb____r.
4. Registration is on T____esday, Jan____ary 13, and Th____rsday, Jan____ary 15.
5. The p____rty is on S____turd____y, M____y 23.

UNIT
5 How Much Is It?

LESSON 1 VOCABULARY

A **Match the words with the picture.**

4 penny	____ nickel	____ bills
____ dime	____ quarter	____ dollar
____ coins	____ cents	

B **Look at the list. Match the school supplies to the price.**

b 1. notebook

____ 2. two pencils

____ 3. book

____ 4. binder

a. 99¢

b. $3

c. 80¢

d. $10

Notebook	$3
Two pencils	80¢
Book	$10
Binder	99¢

A **Look at the picture. Complete the sentences. Use the words in the box.**

shirt ~~sweater~~ pants socks cheap expensive

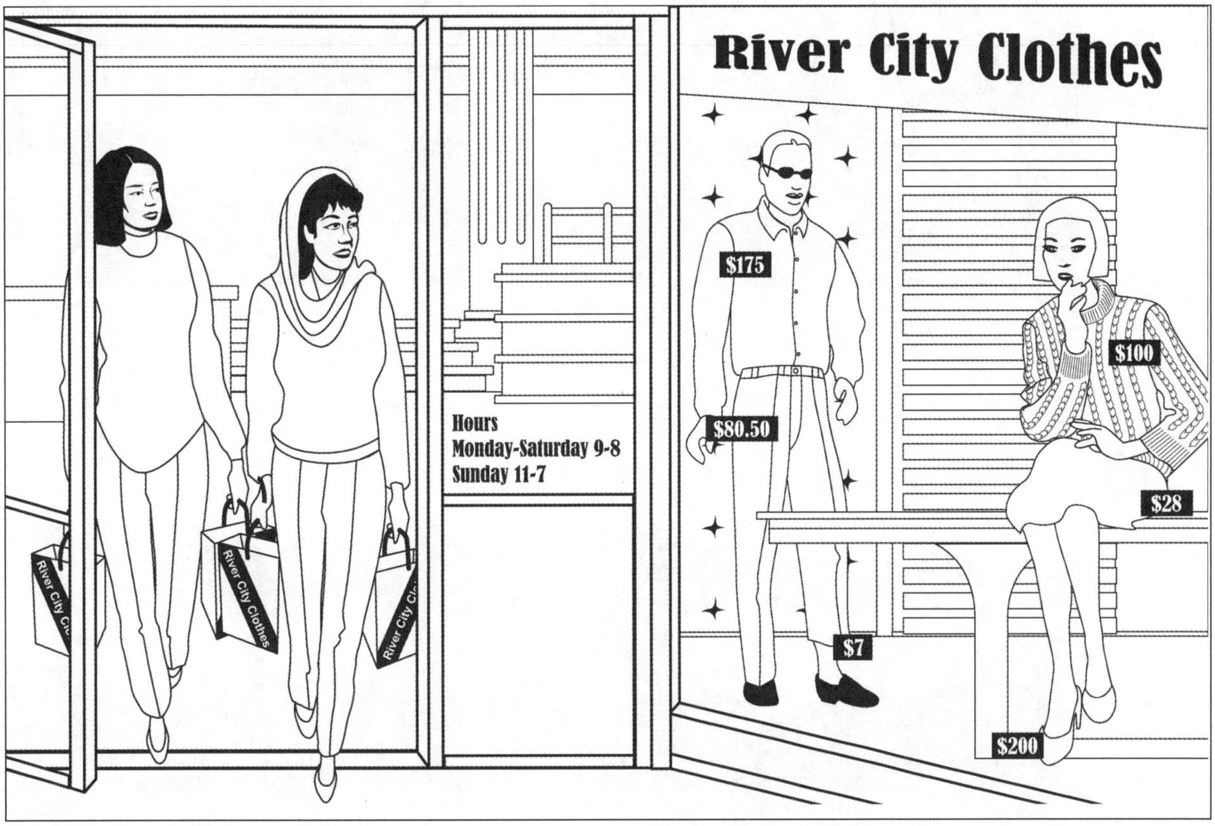

1. The ___sweater___ is $100.
2. The __________ are $80.50.
3. The __________ are $7.
4. The __________ is $175.
5. The shoes are __________.
6. The skirt is __________.

B **Look at the picture in A. Circle *yes* or *no*.**

1. The store is River City Clothes. (yes) no
2. The women are at home. yes no
3. The store is open on Sundays. yes no
4. The shoes are cheap. yes no

A **Look at the pictures. Complete the sentences. Use *This* or *That*.**

1. ___This___ shirt is $10.
2. __________ shirt is $20.
3. __________ book is $21.95.
4. __________ book is $16.

B **Complete the sentences. Circle *a* or *b*.**

1. ____ computer is $450.

   (a.) This b. That

3. ____ computer is $500.

   a. This b. That

2. ____ notebook is $1.75.

   a. This b. That

4. ____ notebook is $2.

   a. This b. That

C Look at the pictures. Write sentences. Use *These* or *Those* and the words in parentheses.

1. ($35) These pants are $35.
2. ($80) ______
3. (expensive) ______

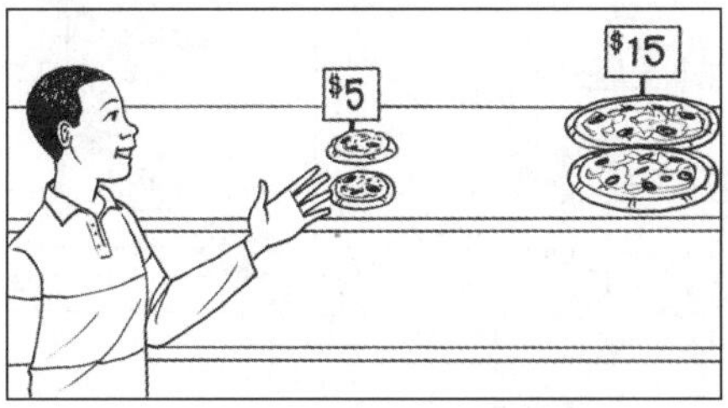

4. ($5) ______
5. (cheap) ______
6. ($15) ______

D Match the pictures and the sentences.

a

b

c

d

e

f

c 1. These shoes are $30.
____ 2. Those shoes are $86.50.
____ 3. These chairs are $199.
____ 4. Those chairs are $250.
____ 5. These clocks are $34.99.
____ 6. Those clocks are $58.

E Complete the sentences. Circle the correct word.

1. (That / Those) student is from Mexico.
2. (This / These) pens are 50¢.
3. (That / Those) sweaters are expensive.
4. (This / These) English class is on Monday.
5. (That / Those) socks are $2.

A Complete the conversation. Use the words and price in the box.

Yes about It's Thanks ~~pants~~

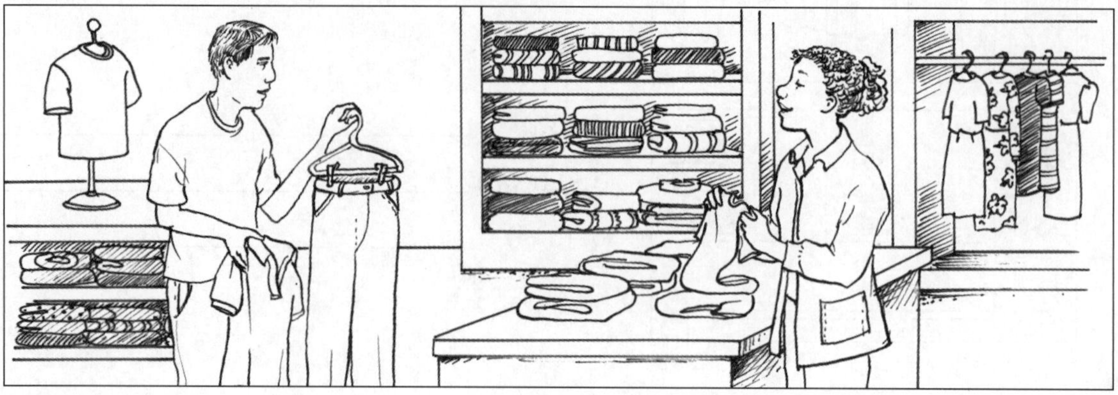

Arun: Excuse me. Are these ___pants___(1) on sale?

Sharon: ________(2), they are.

Arun: How ________(3) this shirt?

Sharon: ________(4) 50% off.

Arun: ________(5).

B Match the questions with the answers.

__b__ 1. Is this brush on sale?

____ 2. Are these pencils on sale?

____ 3. How much are they?

a. They're $2.99.

b. No, it's not.

c. Yes, they are.

C Answer the questions.

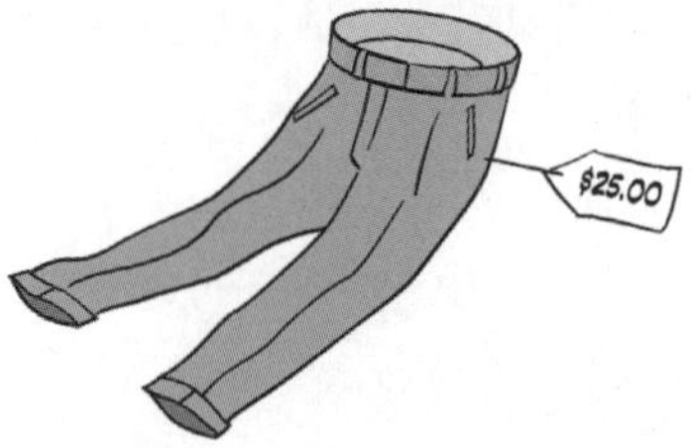

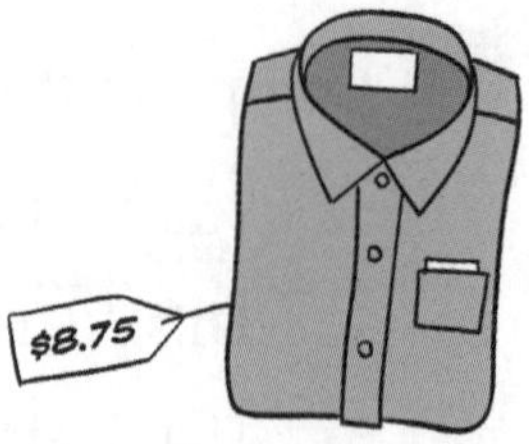

1. How much are the pants?
   They're $25.00.
2. How much are the shoes?
   ____
3. How much is the shirt?
   ____

DO THE MATH Go to page 88.

A **Read the check.**

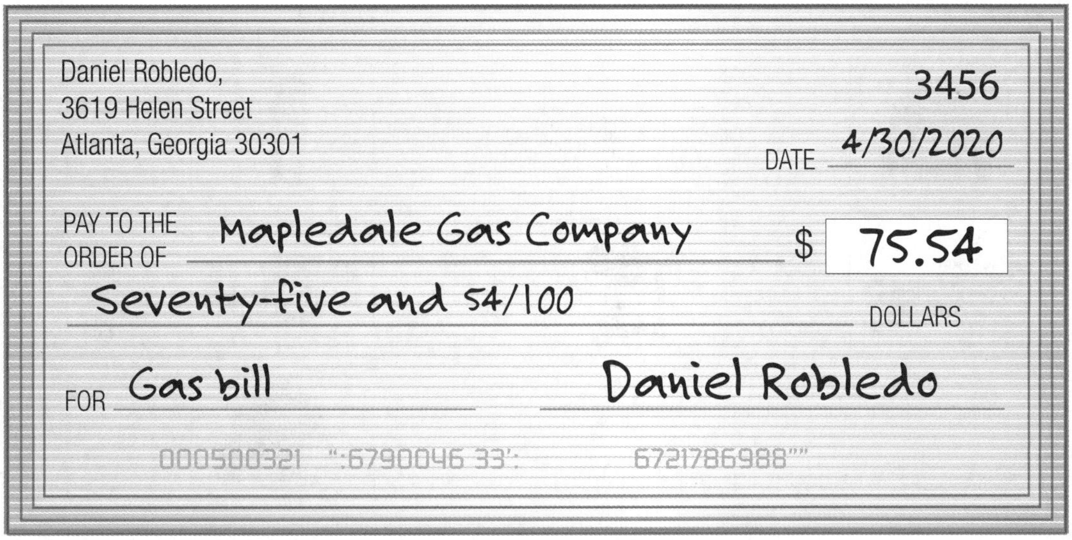
Daniel Robledo,
3619 Helen Street
Atlanta, Georgia 30301

3456

DATE 4/30/2020

PAY TO THE ORDER OF Mapledale Gas Company $ 75.54

Seventy-five and 54/100 DOLLARS

FOR Gas bill

Daniel Robledo

000500321 ":6790046 33": 6721786988""

B **Look at the picture in A. Complete the sentences. Circle *a* or *b*.**

1. His _____ is $75.54.
   (a.) gas bill b. electric bill
2. The date is _____.
   a. April 30, 2020 b. January 30, 2020
3. The bill is from _____.
   a. Daniel Robledo b. Mapledale Gas Company
4. The amount due is _____.
   a. 3456 b. $75.54
5. The signature is _____.
   a. Daniel Robledo b. gas bill
6. Daniel lives at _____.
   a. 3619 Georgia Street b. 3619 Helen Street
7. The zip code is _____.
   a. 30301 b. 54100
8. The check number is _____.
   a. 2020 b. 3456

Look at the pictures. Complete the crossword puzzle.

Across

2. 

7. 

4. 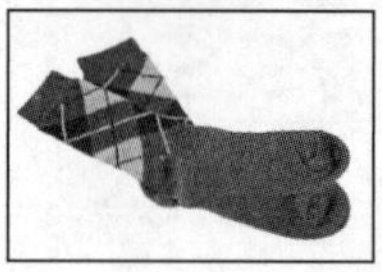

9. 

Down

1. 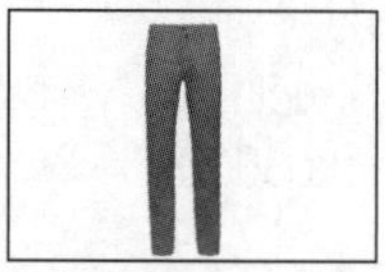

5. 

2. 

6. 

3. 

8. 

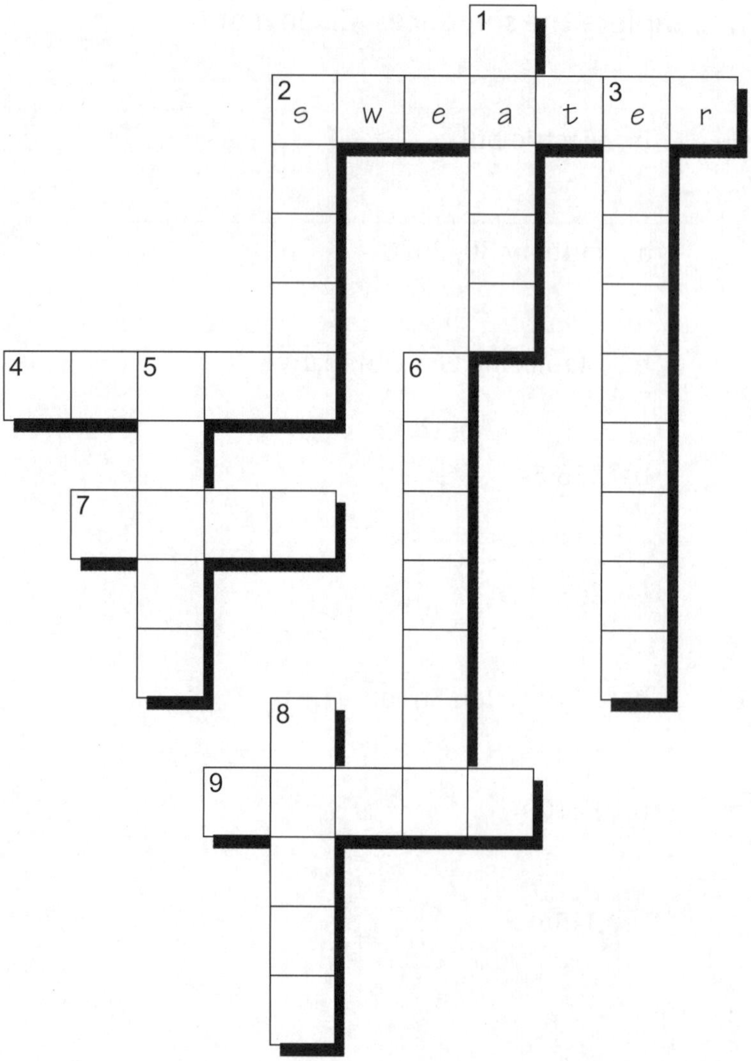

UNIT 6

That's My Son

LESSON 1 VOCABULARY

A **Look at the picture. Write the missing letters.**

1. h __u__ s __b__ __a__ __n__ d
2. w ____ ____ e
3. g ____ ____ l
4. b ____ ____
5. m ____ ____ h ____ ____
6. f ____ ____ ____ e ____
7. b ____ ____ ____
8. p ____ r ____ ____ ____ ____
9. f ____ ____ ____ ____ d

B **Look at the chart. Circle *yes* or *no*.**

1. Is Gloria the mother? yes (no)
2. Is Joel the father? yes no
3. Is Debbie the baby? yes no
4. Is Sam the friend? yes no

Name	Family Member
Joel	father
Debbie	mother
Gloria	baby
Sam	friend

A **Look at the pictures. Complete the sentences. Use the words in the box.**

daughter	son	~~children~~	sister	brother

1. These are my ____children____.
2. This is my ________________. He's ten years old.
3. This is my ________________. She's six years old.
4. That's my ________________. She's married.
5. That's my ________________. He's single.

B **Look at the picture in A. Circle *yes* or *no*.**

1. Are Ivan and Alma divorced? yes (no)
2. Is George ten years old? yes no
3. Is Alma the wife? yes no
4. Is Ivan six years old? yes no

A **Look at the picture. Complete the sentences. Use *his, her,* or *their*.**

1. It's ___his___ book.
2. It's __________ ID.
3. It's __________ money.
4. It's __________ phone number.
5. It's __________ pen.

B **Complete the sentences. Circle *a* or *b*.**

1. This is my brother. ____ name is Tom.

   (a.) His b. Her

2. She is in my class. ____ name is Ana.

   a. His b. Her

3. My name is Carlos. What is ____ name?

   a. your b. my

4. They are my friends. ____ names are Mel and Sandy.

   a. Our b. Their

5. We are husband and wife. ____ names are Mr. and Mrs. Wong.

   a. Our b. Their

C Complete the conversations. Use the verb *live*.

1. **A:** Is your father in Georgia?

   B: No, he ___lives___ in California.

2. **A:** Are your children in Texas?

   B: Yes, they __________ in Dallas.

3. **A:** Is your friend in Minnesota?

   B: No, she __________ in Haiti.

D Complete the sentences. Use *live* or *lives*.

1. Brigitte ___lives___ in Minnesota.
2. Calvin __________ in Washington.
3. You __________ in San Diego.
4. I __________ in Texas.
5. We __________ in Maple.
6. Mr. and Mrs. Levitt __________ in Clinton.

E Write sentences. Use the simple present.

1. Her / brother / live / in / Florida

   Her brother lives in Florida.

2. Our / parents / live / in / South Korea

   ____

3. My / daughter / live / in / Colorado

   ____

4. His / sister / live / in / North Carolina

   ____

5. Their / mother / live / in / New York

   ____

6. Your / son / live / in / Haiti

   ____

Complete the conversation. Use the words in the box.

~~Who's~~	What's	tall	my	old	feet	name

Tuan: __Who's__ that?
1

Joe: That's ________ son.
2

Tuan: ________ his name?
3

Joe: His ________ is Tony.
4

He lives in Florida.

Tuan: How ________ is he?
5

Joe: He's 5 ________ and 3 inches tall.
6

Tuan: How ________ is he?
7

Joe: He's 10.

DO THE MATH Go to page 89.

LESSON 5 READING

A **Read the note.**

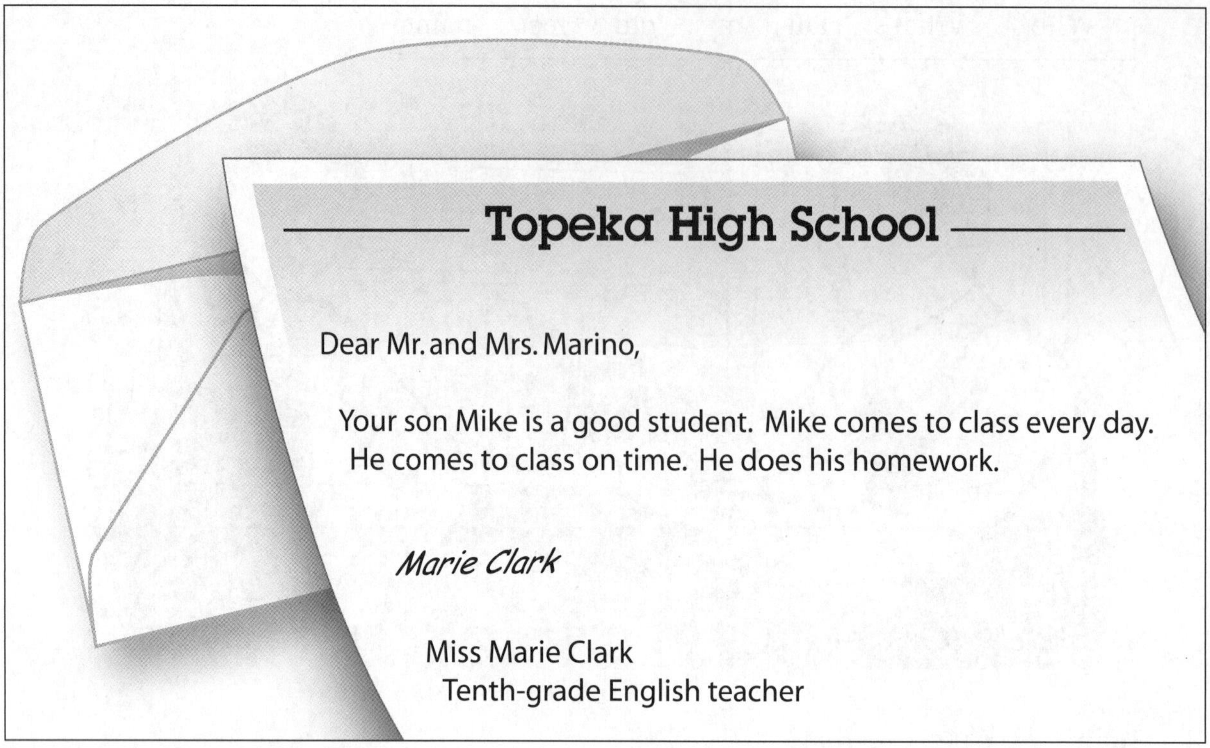

Topeka High School

Dear Mr. and Mrs. Marino,

Your son Mike is a good student. Mike comes to class every day. He comes to class on time. He does his homework.

Marie Clark

Miss Marie Clark
Tenth-grade English teacher

B **Look at the note in A. Complete the sentences.**

1. Miss Clark is a ______tenth______-grade teacher.
2. Mike Marino is in ______________ school.
3. Mike ______________ to class on time.
4. He is a ______________ student.
5. Mike does his ______________.

C **Look at the note. Circle *a* or *b*.**

1. Marie Clark is the ______.

   a. mother (b.) teacher

2. Mr. Marino is the ______.

   a. father b. son

3. Mike is in ______.

   a. middle school b. high school

A Complete the sentences. Use the words in the box.

~~parents~~	baby	sister	single	every day	lives	Mrs.	friend	wife

Across

2. My mother and father are my ___parents___.
5. ________ Vega is a student.
7. Her son ________ in Atlanta.
8. This is my ________, and these are our children.
9. Mike comes to school ________.

Down

1. The ________ is three months old.
3. Silvia is ________.
4. Greg is my ________.
6. They are brother and ________.

B Write the words in the crossword puzzle.

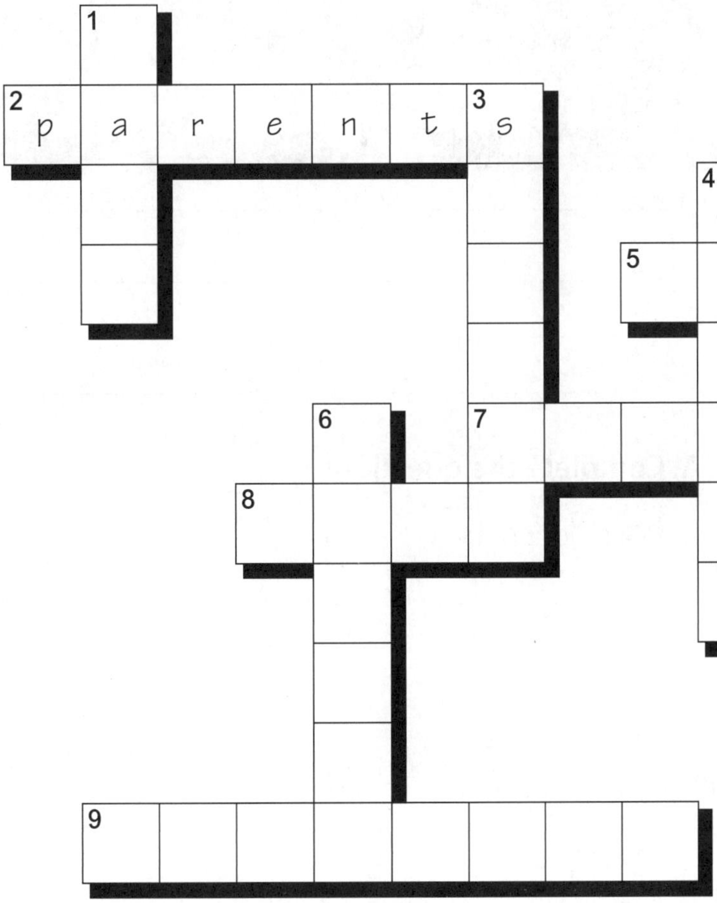

UNIT 7
Do We Need Apples?

LESSON 1 VOCABULARY

A **Match the words with the pictures. Use the words in the box.**

apples	~~bananas~~	broccoli	fruit	cabbage
corn	grapes	vegetables	oranges	

1. bananas
2. ____________
3. ____________
4. ____________
5. ____________
6. ____________
7. ____________
8. ____________
9. ____________

B **Look at the picture in A. Complete the questions.**

1. **A:** How much is the broccoli?
   B: It's $1.30.
2. **A:** How much are the ____________?
   B: They're $1.20.
3. **A:** How much are the ____________?
   B: They're 50¢.
4. **A:** How much is the ____________?
   B: It's 45¢.

A **Look at the picture. Complete the sentences. Use the words in the box.**

rice	beef	chicken	~~lamb~~	vegetables

1. The father likes ___lamb___.
2. The mother likes ________________.
3. The daughter likes ________________.
4. The son likes ________________.
5. They all like ________________.

B **Complete the chart. Use the words in the box.**

~~broccoli~~	~~apples~~	~~beef~~	oranges	lamb
corn	bananas	chicken	cabbage	

Fruit	Vegetables	Meat
apples	broccoli	beef

A **Complete the sentences. Use *don't* or *doesn't*.**

1. My parents ___don't___ like pizza.
2. They ________________ like cheese.
3. She ________________ like milk.
4. The children ________________ like meat.
5. He ________________ like vegetables.
6. Her daughter ________________ like rice.

B **Complete the sentences. Circle *a* or *b*.**

1. Lonnie ____ apples.
   (a.) doesn't like   b. don't like
2. Mrs. Martinez ____ milk.
   a. doesn't like   b. don't like
3. Mr. and Mrs. Jones ____ broccoli.
   a. doesn't like   b. don't like
4. I ____ bananas.
   a. doesn't like   b. don't like
5. He ____ corn.
   a. doesn't like   b. don't like
6. You ____ cabbage.
   a. doesn't like   b. don't like

C **Write new sentences. Use *don't* or *doesn't*.**

1. You like pork. ___You don't like pork.___
2. We like cabbage. ________________
3. The teacher likes fruit. ________________
4. I like lamb. ________________
5. The boy likes bread. ________________

D Complete the conversations. Use *do* or *does*.

1. **A:** Do we need eggs?

   B: Yes, we ___do___.

2. **A:** Does she need fruit?

   B: Yes, she ______.

3. **A:** Do you need beef?

   B: Yes, I ______.

4. **A:** Do they need vegetables?

   B: Yes, they ______.

5. **A:** Does he need corn?

   B: Yes, he ______.

E Match the questions with the answers.

_d_ 1. Does Alonso need a notebook?

___ 2. Does Tina need pencils?

___ 3. Do we need apples?

___ 4. Do I need bread?

___ 5. Do Mr. and Mrs. Winters need rice?

a. No, they don't.

b. No, she doesn't.

c. Yes, you do.

d. No, he doesn't.

e. No, we don't.

F Unscramble the sentences.

1. grapes / doesn't / Raja / like

   Raja doesn't like grapes.

2. need / students / The / English dictionary / an

   ______

3. Reza / Ms. / oranges / needs

   ______

4. in / live / don't / We / Washington

   ______

5. children / eggs / The / like / don't

   ______

6. like / don't / chicken / You

   ______

A Put the conversation in the correct order.

____ **Fatima:** Thanks.

____ **Paul:** Here you go.

__1__ **Fatima:** Excuse me. I need milk and eggs.

____ **Paul:** You're welcome.

B Put the conversation in the correct order.

____ **Marcos:** How much are they?

____ **Paul:** They're right here.

__1__ **Marcos:** Excuse me. Where are the apples?

____ **Paul:** They're $1.50.

DO THE MATH Go to page 90.

A Read the shopping list.

B Look at A. Circle *yes* or *no*.

1. Does Mrs. Ma need oranges? (yes) no
2. Does she need six bottles of water? yes no
3. Does she need four pounds of chicken? yes no
4. Does she need five cans of soup? yes no
5. Does Mrs. Ma need beef? yes no
6. Does she need one box of tea? yes no

C Complete the sentences. Use words from the list in A.

1. Mrs. Ma needs two boxes of ___cereal___.
2. She needs three pounds of ______________.
3. She needs two pounds of ______________.
4. Mrs. Ma needs ______________ bottles of water.
5. She needs ______________ pound of cheese.
6. She needs ______________ cans of soup.

Look at the pictures. Complete the crossword puzzle.

Across

2. 

6. 

5. 

8. 

Down

1. 

7. 

3. 

9. 

4. 

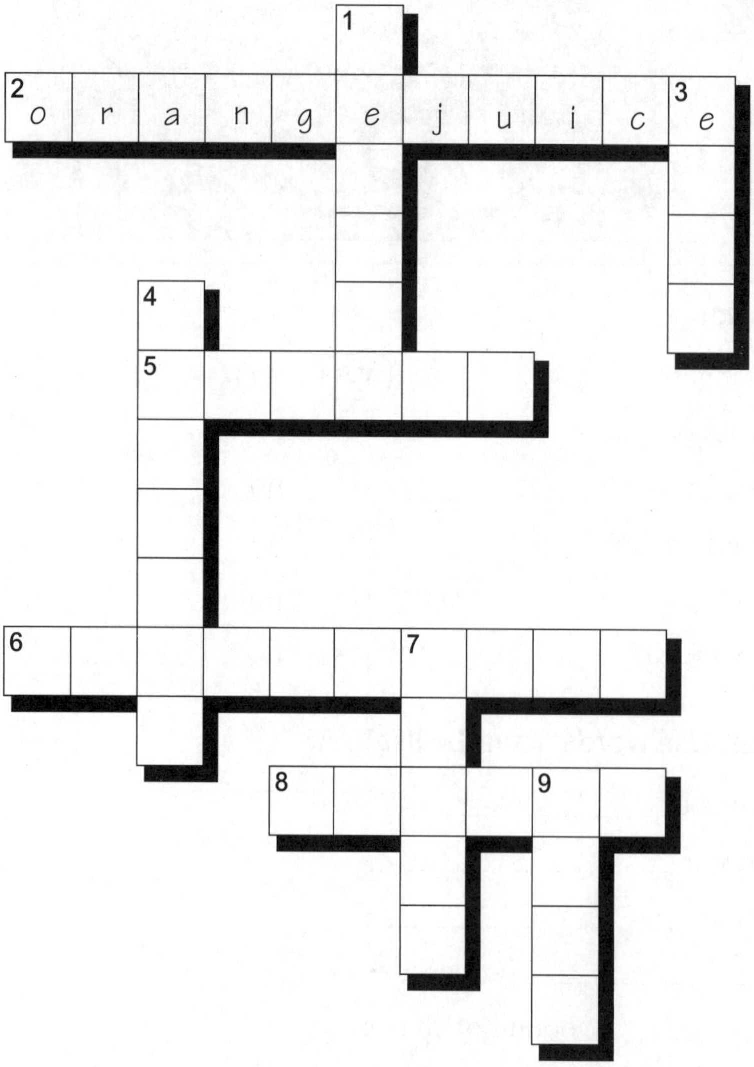

UNIT

8 What's the Matter?

LESSON 1 VOCABULARY

A Look at the picture. Write the missing letters.

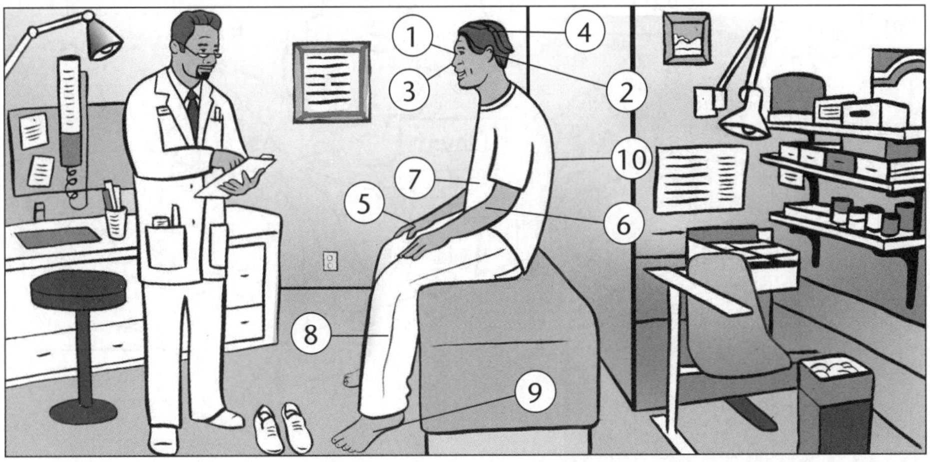

1. e _y_ e
2. e ____ r
3. n ____ s ____
4. h e ____ ____
5. h a ____ ____
6. a ____ ____
7. s ____ ____ ____ ____ c ____
8. l ____ ____
9. f ____ ____ ____
10. b ____ ____ k

B Look at the form. Circle *yes* or *no*.

MIDTOWN CLINIC REGISTRATION FORM

Name: Jain, Arun
last name first name

Address: 7690 Walnut Street Chicago, Illinois 60602

Phone number: (312) 555-2390 Age: 52

☐ Married ☐ Single ☒ Divorced

How are you feeling? Fine

1. His first name is Arun. (yes) no
2. His address is 60602 Walnut Street. yes no
3. His phone number is (312) 555-2390. yes no

A Look at the picture. Match the person to the health problem.

_e_ 1. Alicia	a. headache
____ 2. David	b. sore throat
____ 3. Mrs. Laurent	c. fever
____ 4. Mr. Laurent	d. stomachache
____ 5. Barbara	e. cough
____ 6. Patrick	f. earache

B Look at the picture in A. Circle *yes* or *no*.

1. Barbara has a stomachache.	(yes)	no
2. Mr. Laurent has the flu.	yes	no
3. David has a fever.	yes	no
4. Mrs. Laurent has an earache.	yes	no
5. Alicia has a cough.	yes	no
6. Patrick has an earache.	yes	no

A **Look at the pictures. Write two sentences about each picture. Use *has* or *have* and the words in parentheses.**

1. (I) I have a sore throat.
2. (You) ______________________

3. (She) ______________________
4. (He) ______________________

5. (We) ______________________
6. (They) ______________________

B **Complete the sentences. Use *has* or *have*.**

1. His daughter ___has___ an earache.
2. Her son ______________ the flu.
3. The teacher and the students ______________ fevers.
4. My mother ______________ a cough.
5. Annie and Daniela ______________ sore throats.
6. Their friend ______________ a headache.

C Match the questions with the answers.

c	1. Does Patricia have a book?	a. No, they don't.
____	2. Do Donna and Marcus have children?	b. Yes, we do.
____	3. Does Azim have a credit card?	c. No, she doesn't.
____	4. Do you have $20?	d. No, he doesn't.
____	5. Do we have apples?	e. Yes, I do.

D Complete the conversations. Use *does* or *do*.

1. **A:** Does he have an earache? **B:** Yes, he ____does____.
2. **A:** Does she have a sore throat? **B:** Yes, she ____________.
3. **A:** Do I have a fever? **B:** Yes, you ____________.
4. **A:** Do they have the flu? **B:** Yes, they ____________.

E Write questions. Use *do* or *does, have,* and the words in parentheses.

1. (she, sweater) ____Does she have a sweater?____
2. (they, eggs) ____________________
3. (you, quarter) ____________________
4. (he, car) ____________________
5. (we, paper) ____________________

F Complete the questions and answers. Use *do, does, have,* or *has.*

1. **A:** ____Does____ Nancy have a fever?
   B: No, she ____has____ an earache.
2. **A:** ____________ he have a stomachache?
   B: No, he ____________ a headache.
3. **A:** ____________ Mr. and Mrs. Chavez have the flu?
   B: No, they ____________ colds.
4. **A:** ____________ you have a cough?
   B: No, I ____________ a sore throat.
5. **A:** ____________ I have the flu?
   B: No, you ____________ a cold.

LESSON 4 EVERYDAY CONVERSATION

A Complete the conversation. Use the words and time in the box.

thank	11:00	name	flu	doctor	Rosita	matter	~~Hello~~

Receptionist: Hello (1), River City Clinic.

Adolfo: This is Adolfo Flores. My daughter needs to see the ______ (2).

Receptionist: What's the ______ (3)?

Adolfo: She has the ______ (4).

Receptionist: What's her ______ (5)?

Adolfo: Her name is ______ (6). She's seven months old.

Receptionist: Is ______ (7) OK?

Adolfo: Yes, ______ (8) you.

B Circle the words that start with *s*.

A: Hi, (Sharon.) Are you at (school?)

B: No, I'm at the clinic in Springfield.

A: Are you sick?

B: Yes, I have a stomachache.

A: Oh, I'm sorry.

B: Thanks. See you next Saturday.

DO THE MATH Go to page 91.

A Read the forms.

1
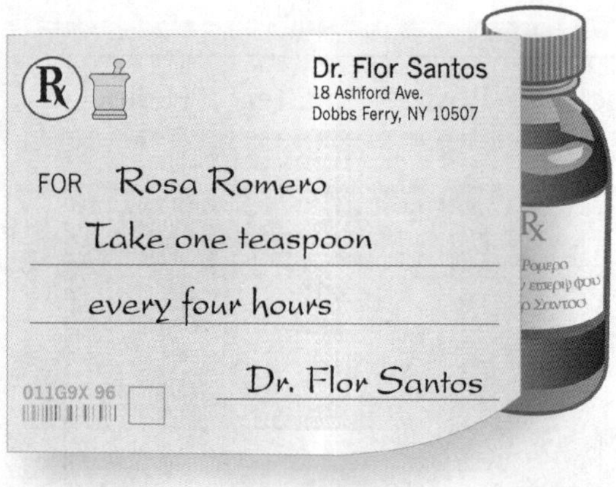
Dr. Flor Santos
18 Ashford Ave.
Dobbs Ferry, NY 10507
FOR Rosa Romero
Take one teaspoon
every four hours
Dr. Flor Santos
011G9X 96

2
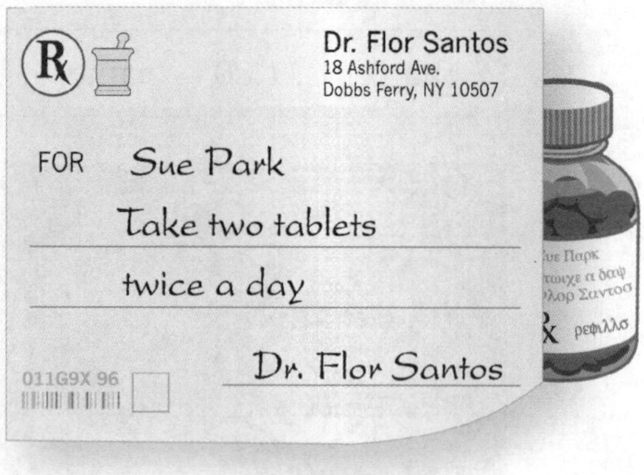
Dr. Flor Santos
18 Ashford Ave.
Dobbs Ferry, NY 10507
FOR Sue Park
Take two tablets
twice a day
Dr. Flor Santos
011G9X 96

3

Dr. Flor Santos
18 Ashford Ave.
Dobbs Ferry, NY 10507
FOR Charlie Prajak
Take one tablespoon
every day
Dr. Flor Santos
011G9X 96

4
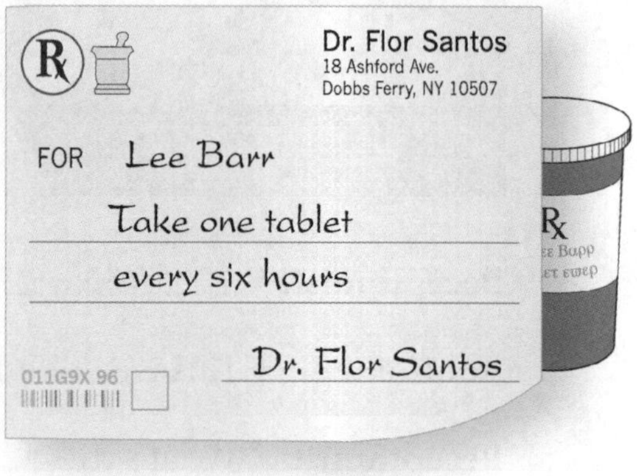
Dr. Flor Santos
18 Ashford Ave.
Dobbs Ferry, NY 10507
FOR Lee Barr
Take one tablet
every six hours
Dr. Flor Santos
011G9X 96

B Look at A. Circle *a* or *b*.

1. Medicine 1:
   a. take two teaspoons   b. take one teaspoon
2. Medicine 2:
   a. take three times a day   b. take twice a day
3. Medicine 2:
   a. take two tablets   b. take one tablet
4. Medicine 3:
   a. take one tablespoon   b. take one teaspoon
5. Medicine 4:
   a. take every four hours   b. take every six hours
6. Medicine 4:
   a. take six tablets   b. take one tablet

A Complete the words in each sentence with one letter. Use the letters in the box.

~~a~~ e i o u

1. Wh__a__t's the m__a__tter?
2. Take tw____ tablesp____ ____ns every f____ur h____urs.
3. We have med____c____ne for colds.
4. I n____ ____d to s____ ____ th____ doctor.
5. Do yo____ have the fl____?

B Look at the pictures. Match the pictures to the sentences.

a
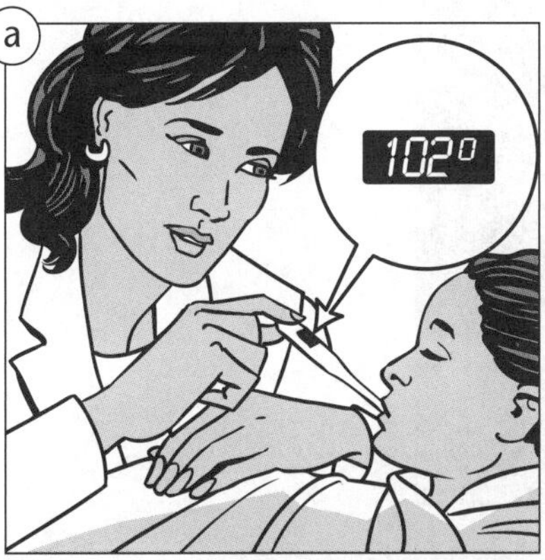

b

c

d
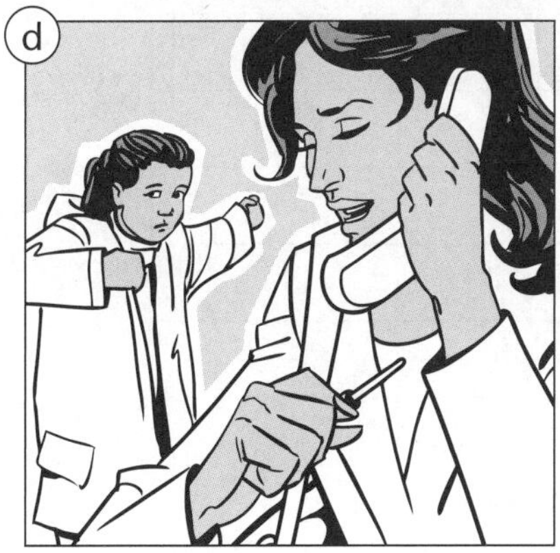

e

__a__ 1. "You have a fever."

____ 2. "Is 1:00 OK?"

____ 3. "Hello. My daughter needs to see the doctor."

____ 4. "Your daughter has the flu."

____ 5. "Yes, thank you. Goodbye."

UNIT 9

What Size?

LESSON 1 VOCABULARY

A **Complete the chart. Use the words in the box.**

~~orange~~	~~pants~~	socks	shirt	purple	red	shoes	green

Colors	Clothes
orange	*pants*

B **Complete the color words. Write the missing letters.**

1. p _u_ _r_ p _l_ e
2. w ___ ___ ___ e
3. g ___ ___ ___ ___
4. o ___ ___ n ___ ___
5. b ___ ___ ___
6. r ___ ___
7. y ___ ___ ___ o ___
8. b ___ ___ w ___
9. b ___ ___ c ___

LESSON 2 WRITING

A **Look at the pictures. Complete the sentences. Use the words in the box.**

boots ~~shorts~~ cap jacket dress belt

1. **Matt:** I'm wearing ___shorts___.
2. **Greg:** I'm wearing a ________________.

3. **Nancy:** It's a ________________.
4. **Selma:** It's a ________________.

5. **Tina:** I'm wearing ________________.
6. **Paul:** It's a new ________________.

B **Look at the pictures in A. Circle *yes* or *no*.**

1. Matt is wearing a cap.	yes	(no)
2. Greg is wearing shorts.	yes	no
3. Nancy is wearing pants.	yes	no
4. Selma is wearing a jacket.	yes	no
5. Tina is wearing a coat.	yes	no
6. Paul is wearing a sweater.	yes	no

A Complete the sentences. Use *am, is,* or *are.*

1. He ___is___ wearing a brown sweater.
2. You __________ wearing a purple T-shirt.
3. Anita __________ wearing a white coat.
4. We __________ wearing green jackets.
5. I __________ wearing a black dress.
6. Norma and Chang Sun __________ wearing blue caps.

B Look at the pictures. Write three sentences about each picture. Use *is wearing* or *are wearing* and the words in parentheses.

1. (boots) ___She is wearing boots.___
2. (coat) ____________________
3. (pants) ____________________

4. (T-shirts) ____________________
5. (shorts) ____________________
6. (caps) ____________________

C Complete the sentences. Circle *a* or *b*.

1. You ____ wearing a brown jacket.
   (a.) are b. is
2. I ____ wearing a red T-shirt.
   a. is b. am
3. He ____ wearing black pants.
   a. is b. am
4. They ____ wearing blue boots.
   a. are b. is
5. He ____ wearing a blue coat.
   a. am b. is
6. We ____ wearing green shoes.
   a. are b. is
7. You ____ wearing a yellow shirt.
   a. is b. are
8. They ____ wearing red hats.
   a. are b. am

D Complete the conversations. Use *Is* or *Are*.

1. **A:** ___Is___ she reading a book?
   B: Yes, she is.
2. **A:** ________ he going to the clinic?
   B: No, he's not.
3. **A:** ________ the cat sleeping?
   B: No, it's not.
4. **A:** ________ you wearing a coat?
   B: No, I'm not.
5. **A:** ________ they going to school?
   B: Yes, they are.

E Answer the questions. Circle *a* or *b*.

1. Is Claire wearing a purple dress?
   (a.) Yes, she is. b. Yes, you are.
2. Are the students doing their homework?
   a. Yes, she is. b. No, they're not.
3. Is Mr. Foss sleeping?
   a. Yes, he is. b. Yes, she is.
4. Are we wearing sweaters?
   a. No, we're not. b. No, they're not.
5. Are you going to the store?
   a. Yes, I am. b. Yes, you are.

F Write sentences. Use the present continuous.

1. We / read / the books
   We are reading the books.
2. Lila / sleep
   ____
3. He / wear / black / shoes
   ____
4. They / go / to / a party
   ____

A **Put the conversation in the correct order.**

____ **Eva:** Medium.

____ **Clerk:** What size?

__1__ **Eva:** I'm looking for a dress.

____ **Eva:** Thanks.

____ **Clerk:** Here's a medium.

B **Fill in the blanks with colors. Circle the items you are wearing.**

I'm wearing a ____________ shirt/sweater/dress.

I'm wearing (a) ____________ pants/skirt/shorts.

I'm wearing ____________ boots/shoes.

I'm (not) wearing a ____________ cap.

DO THE MATH Go to page 92.

A Read the weather report.

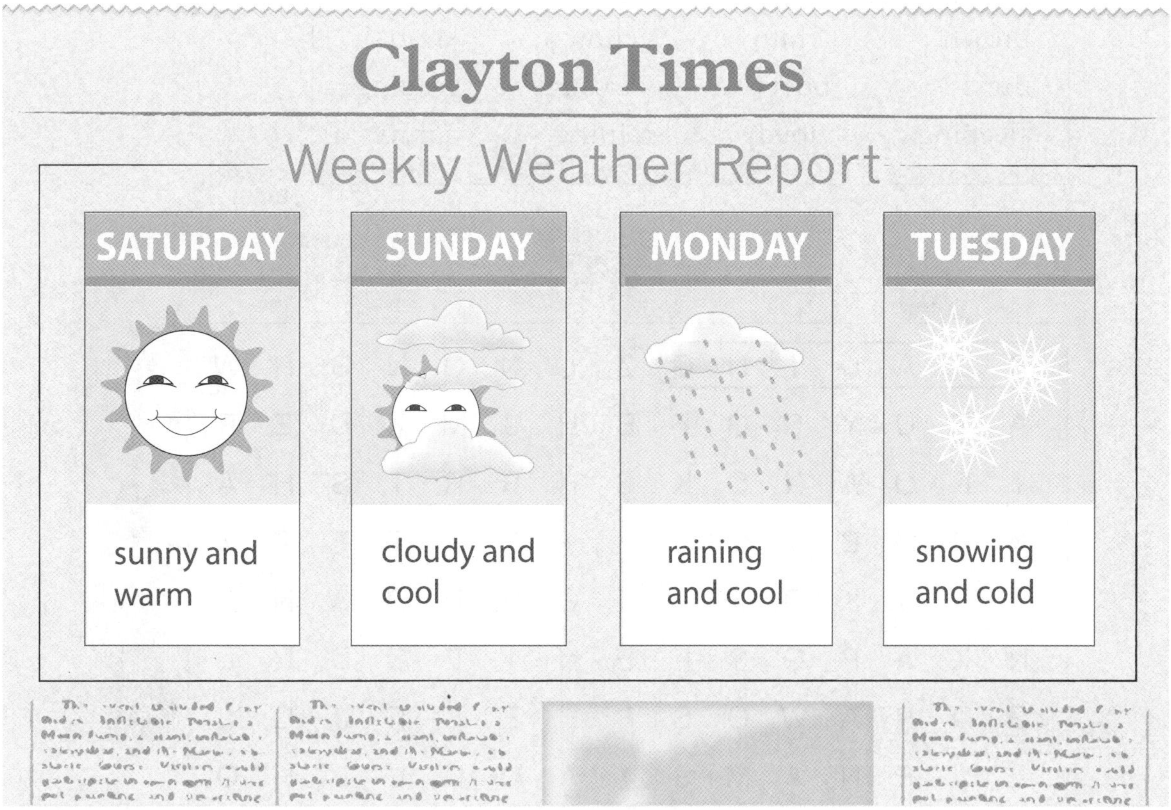

B Look at A. Circle *a* or *b*.

1. Saturday
   (a.) sunny b. cloudy
2. Saturday
   a. warm b. hot
3. Sunday
   a. sunny b. cloudy
4. Monday
   a. warm b. cool
5. Monday
   a. snowing b. raining
6. Tuesday
   a. snowing b. raining

C Complete the sentences. Use words from the weather report in A.

1. Saturday: ____sunny____ and warm.
2. Sunday: cloudy and ________________.
3. Monday: ________________ and cool.
4. Tuesday: snowing and ________________.

Circle the words in the puzzle. Use the words in the box.

brown	white	yellow	shorts
dress	boots	wearing	~~reading~~
sleeping	cloudy	raining	sunny

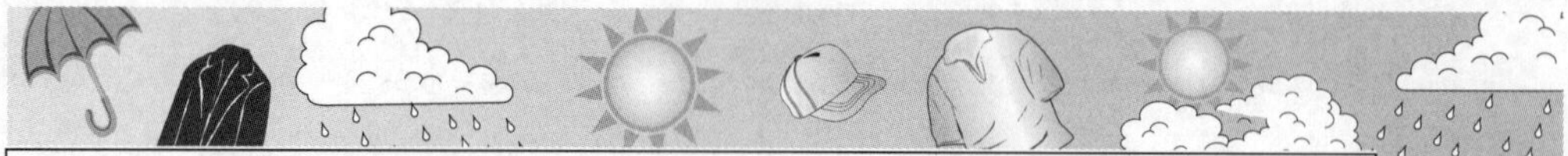

R	E	A	D	I	N	G	Z	L	N	G	N	B	R	W
A	T	U	Y	R	G	F	B	H	J	M	X	D	E	R
I	P	Q	W	X	C	K	S	H	R	R	T	S	H	A
N	P	M	B	T	O	D	L	I	E	A	T	E	Z	Y
I	L	J	K	D	E	R	E	G	B	R	O	W	N	E
N	X	A	P	O	S	E	E	N	I	E	C	D	R	L
G	D	R	A	W	O	S	P	H	F	F	E	J	S	L
L	U	E	N	A	M	S	I	A	N	U	L	L	H	O
S	R	I	B	D	N	O	N	S	W	C	E	S	O	W
G	W	E	A	R	I	N	G	A	L	C	I	T	R	A
L	H	A	N	U	F	E	R	I	C	L	V	E	T	S
E	I	D	N	S	E	H	T	J	B	O	O	T	S	O
N	T	I	O	J	N	O	I	S	C	U	T	R	E	S
N	E	R	R	T	D	O	N	I	G	D	A	R	I	M
L	A	P	E	S	U	N	N	Y	E	Y	N	A	V	Y

UNIT

10 This Is My Home

LESSON 1 VOCABULARY

A Match the words with the picture. Use the words in the box.

stove	TV	sofa	~~window~~	room
furniture	refrigerator	bed	dresser	

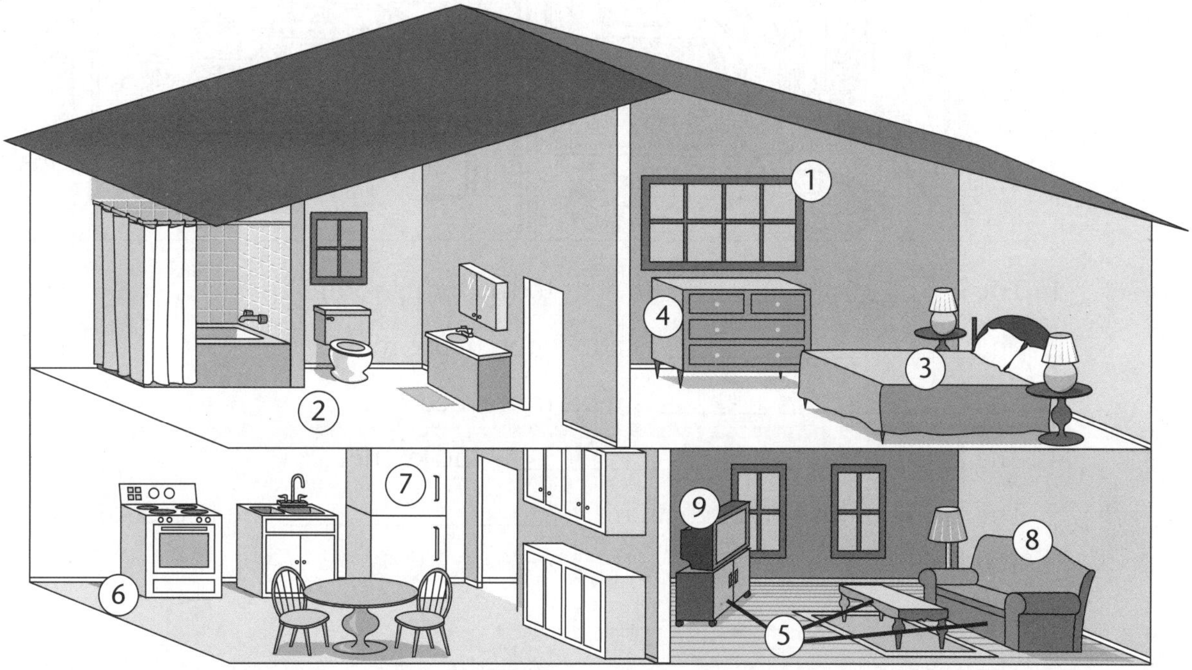

1. window
2. ____________
3. ____________
4. ____________
5. ____________
6. ____________
7. ____________
8. ____________
9. ____________

B Look at the picture in A. Circle *yes* or *no*.

1. Is the table between the TV and the sofa? (yes) no
2. Is the stove next to the refrigerator? yes no
3. Is the sofa across from the TV? yes no
4. Is the dresser next to the bed? yes no

A **Look at the picture. Complete the sentences. Use the words in the box.**

garage	below	above	in	bedroom	bathroom	on	~~kitchen~~

1. The ___kitchen___ is next to the living room.
2. The ____________ is above the living room.
3. The ____________ is next to the bedroom.
4. The bathroom is ____________ the kitchen.
5. The living room and kitchen are ____________ the bedroom and bathroom.
6. The car is in the ____________.
7. The food is ____________ the table.
8. Mrs. Garcia is ____________ the living room.

B **Complete the chart. Use the words in the box.**

~~bedroom~~	living room	~~bed~~	kitchen	sofa	stove

Rooms	Furniture
bedroom	bed

LESSON 3 GRAMMAR

A Match the sentences.

d	1. Their living room is small.	a.	Ethan's kitchen is white.
____	2. Their house is old.	b.	Lisa's garage is big.
____	3. Her bathroom is blue.	c.	Mr. and Mrs. Tam's house is old.
____	4. His kitchen is white.	d.	Ed and Elsa's living room is small.
____	5. Her garage is big.	e.	Jane's bathroom is blue.

B Complete the sentences. Use the possessive and the names in parentheses.

1. ______Jia's______ dress is new. (Jia)
2. ____________________ bedroom is red. (Mr. and Mrs. Lim)
3. ____________________ English class is good. (Phu)
4. ____________________ kitchen is nice. (Kara)
5. ____________________ sweater is purple. (Ingrid)

C Look at the picture. Complete the sentences.

1. ____Galina's____ dog is sleeping.
2. ______________ clock is small.
3. ______________ jacket is expensive.
4. ______________ pants are black.

D Complete the questions. Circle *a* or *b*.

1. Matt is ____ the bedroom.

   a. on (b.) in

2. The dog is ____ the sofa.

   a. between b. under

3. My apartment is ____ the second floor.

   a. on b. over

4. The table is ____ the bed and the dresser.

   a. between b. on

E Look at the pictures. Write sentences. Use prepositions *next to* and *between*.

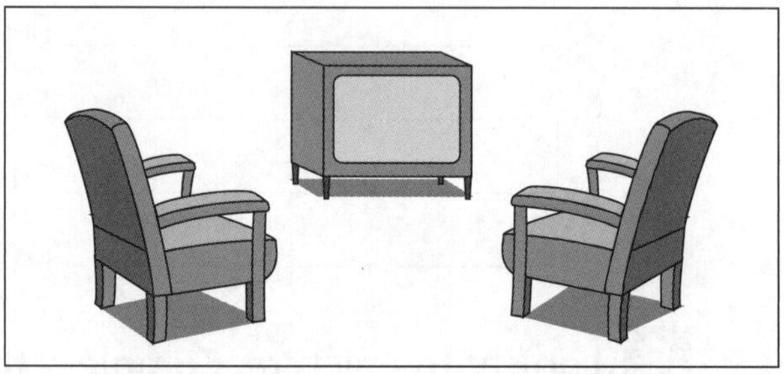

1. The bananas are next to the apple.
2. ______________________________
3. ______________________________
4. ______________________________

F Write sentences. Use the possessive.

1. Mr. and Mrs. Soto / house / is / on the corner

   Mr. and Mrs. Soto's house is on the corner.

2. Peng / living room / has / two / sofas

   ____

3. Orane / calendar / is / black and white

   ____

4. Jerry and Olivia / books / are / expensive

   ____

A **Complete the conversation. Use the words and price in the box.**

there	~~apartment~~	rent	$1,100

Dolores: Is there an apartment (1) for rent?

Mr. Smith: Yes, ____________ (2) is.

Dolores: How much is the ____________ (3)?

Mr. Smith: It's ____________ (4) a month.

B **Put the conversation in the correct order.**

____ **Luke:** It's $1,200 a month.

____ **Jorge:** How much is the rent?

____ **Luke:** Yes, there is.

__1__ **Jorge:** Is there a condo for rent?

DO THE MATH Go to page 92.

A Read the housing ads.

Internet Search

3 BR/3 BA house $1,100 a month
3618 Washington Street
MORE INFO

2 BR/2 BA apartment $850 a month
198 Sixth Street
MORE INFO

Room for rent in my home $425 a month
(240) 555-6795
MORE INFO

2 BR/1 BA duplex $700 a month
9009 Bar Street
(240) 555-83444
MORE INFO

B Look at A. Circle *a* or *b*.

1. How much is the apartment rent?
   a. $425 b. $850
2. How many bedrooms are there in the duplex?
   a. one b. two
3. Where is the house?
   a. Washington Street b. Barr Street
4. How many bathrooms are there in the apartment?
   a. one b. two
5. How much is the room rent?
   a. $425 b. $700

Circle the words in the puzzle. Use the words in the box.

dresser	stove	bedroom	garage
chair	rent	mobile home	window
bathroom	many	apartment	~~kitchen~~

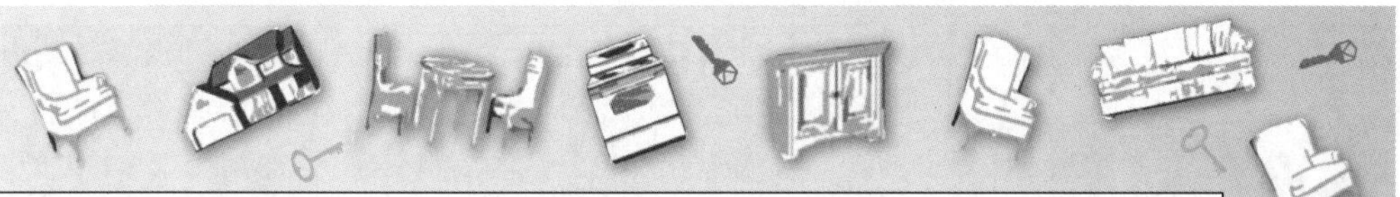

E	I	T	R	A	S	G	N	O	R	W	I	M	N	T
E	S	N	I	D	L	A	R	N	U	F	B	O	C	P
N	O	S	K	R	K	I	T	C	H	E	N	B	D	I
E	T	V	A	E	L	H	C	R	A	M	B	I	Z	O
R	O	M	K	S	O	O	S	T	O	V	E	L	R	B
N	Y	L	E	S	L	A	D	T	S	E	R	E	O	E
I	M	S	L	E	M	I	W	I	N	D	R	H	J	D
E	A	P	A	R	T	M	E	N	T	Y	E	O	W	R
S	U	R	I	S	C	E	X	E	L	S	E	M	Q	O
A	M	A	B	A	T	H	R	O	O	M	P	E	P	O
R	W	O	O	E	R	E	H	W	C	H	A	I	R	M
E	S	I	O	U	Y	W	O	N	K	O	H	W	E	R
N	R	E	T	G	A	R	A	G	E	H	A	H	T	S
T	I	D	R	I	E	O	N	S	L	E	G	G	I	W
S	W	I	N	D	O	W	H	I	S	T	M	A	N	Y

UNIT 11

Where's the Bank?

LESSON 1 VOCABULARY

A **Match the words with the pictures.**

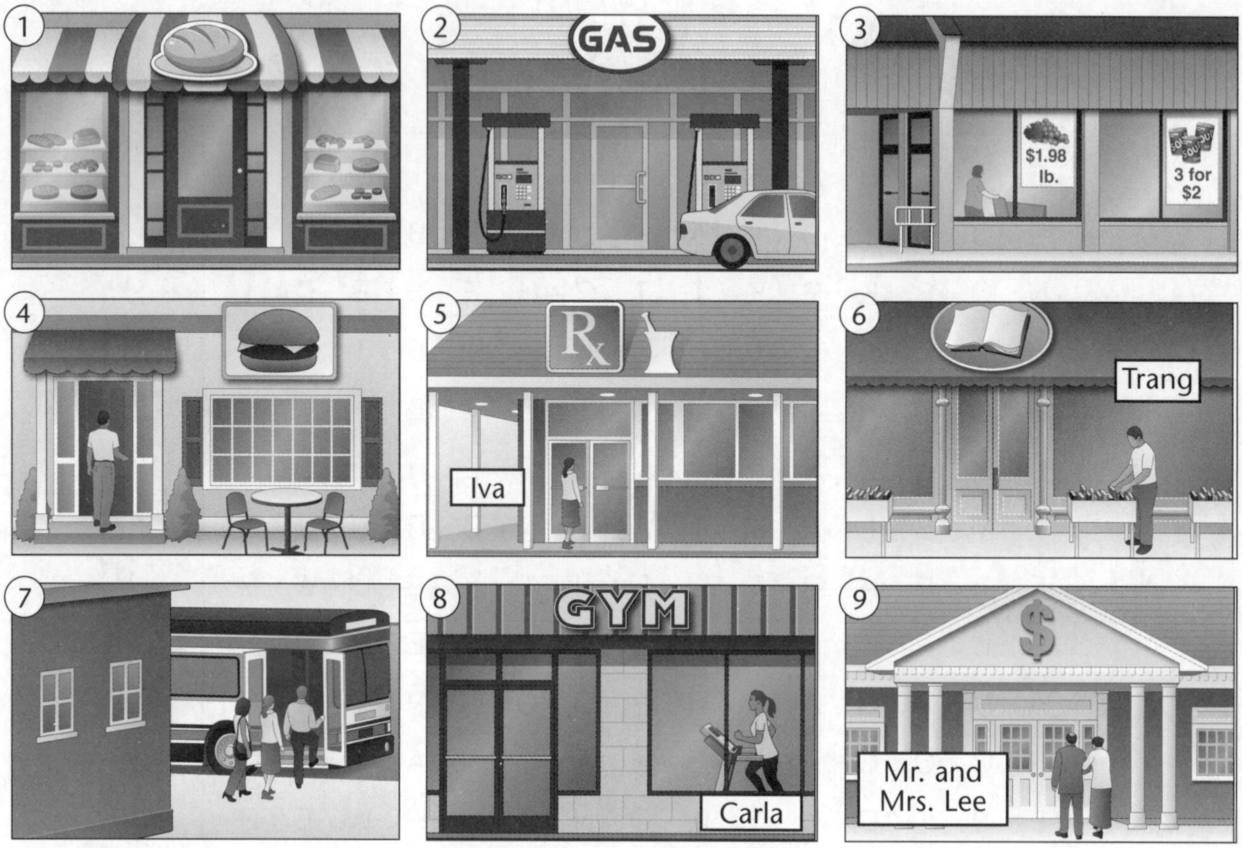

_3_ supermarket	____ bookstore	____ bakery
____ bank	____ restaurant	____ bus station
____ drugstore	____ gym	____ gas station

B **Look at the pictures in A. Complete the sentences. Use the words in the box.**

~~gym~~	bookstore	bank	drugstore

1. Carla is in the ____gym____.
2. Trang is at the ____________.
3. Iva is going to the ____________.
4. Mr. and Mrs. Lee are going to the ____________.

LESSON 2 WRITING

A **Look at the picture. Complete the sentences. Use the words in the box.**

on the corner	restaurant	between	~~apartment building~~	next to	across from

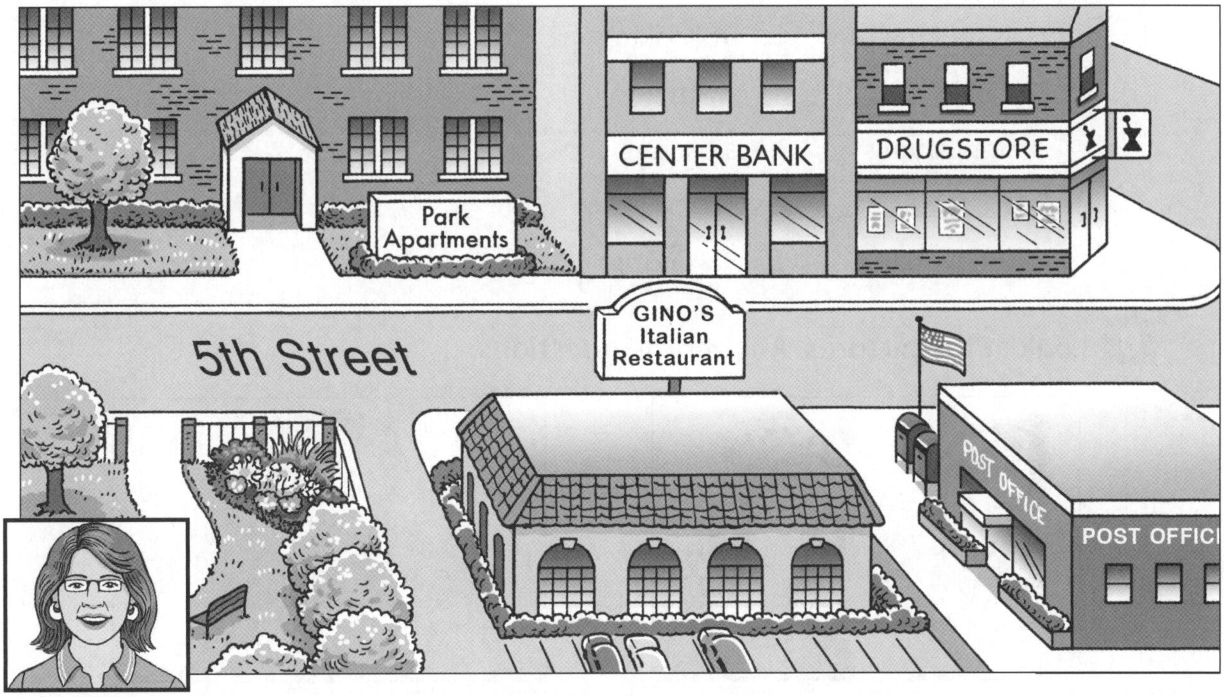

1. This is my apartment building.
2. My apartment building is ________________ the bank.
3. My apartment building is ________________ the park.
4. There's a drugstore ________________.
5. The bank is ________________ my apartment building and the drugstore.
6. There's a ________________ next to the park.

B **Look at the picture in A. Circle *yes* or *no*.**

1. The bank is on the corner. yes (no)
2. There's a supermarket. yes no
3. The park is next to the drugstore. yes no
4. The street is Fifth Street. yes no
5. There's a school. yes no
6. The restaurant is between the park and the post office. yes no

LESSON 3 GRAMMAR

A Complete the sentences. Choose *a* or *b*.

1. He ____________ a new book.
   (a.) is buying   b. are buying
2. They ____________ at a house today.
   a. is looking   b. are looking
3. The baby ____________ with a toy.
   a. are playing   b. is playing
4. She ____________ late today.
   a. are working   b. is working

B Look at the pictures. Answer the questions.

1. What are they doing? (talk)
   They are talking.
2. What is she doing? (drink)
   ____
3. What is he doing? (wash)
   ____

C Look at the picture. Answer the questions.

1. Where are Mr. and Mrs. Huang going?

   They are going to the drugstore.
2. Where are Carlo and his son going? ______
3. What is Julie doing? (buy gas) ______
4. What is Phuong doing? ______

D Read the sentences. Write *Where are you?* or *What are you doing*?

1. I'm at the supermarket.

   Where are you?
2. I'm cooking dinner. ______
3. I'm at the restaurant. ______
4. I'm listening to music. ______
5. I'm exercising at the gym. ______

E Unscramble the sentences.

1. going / bus station / is / he / the / to

   He is going to the bus station.
2. she / next to / gym / walking / is / the

   ______
3. listening / music / are / to / they

   ______
4. children / playing / the / park / in / the / are

   ______

LESSON 4 EVERYDAY CONVERSATION

A Put the conversation in the correct order.

____ **Hector:** Thank you.

____ **Vinh:** You're welcome.

____ **Vinh:** It's between the bank and the bookstore.

__1__ **Hector:** Excuse me. I'm looking for a drugstore.

B Put the conversation in the correct order.

____ **Katrina:** They're using the computers.

____ **Jonas:** What are they doing?

____ **Katrina:** They're at work.

__1__ **Jonas:** Where are they?

DO THE MATH Go to page 93.

A Read the brochure.

SPRING CITY
Important Phone Numbers

Emergency 911

- POLICE
- FIRE
- AMBULANCE AND HOSPITAL

NON-EMERGENCY NUMBERS

COURTHOUSE
5667 Court Street
(702) 555-0095
email address: *court@springcity.gov*

DMV
111 Third Street
(702) 555-7713
email address: *dmv@springcity.gov*

FIRE STATION
2156 Jones Street
(702) 555-0088

HOSPITAL
4545 Pine Street
(702) 555-9834

POLICE STATION
999 First Street
(702) 555-5885

B Complete the sentences. Use the words and numbers from A.

1. For an emergency, call ___911___.
2. The non-emergency number for the ______________ is (702) 555-0088.
3. The non-emergency number for the police station is ______________.
4. The DMV is on ______________ Street.
5. The email address for the courthouse is ______________.
6. The address of the hospital is ______________.
7. The email address for the DMV is ______________.
8. The police station is on ______________ Street.

A Look at the pictures. Match the pictures to the sentences.

a

b

c

d

__b__ 1. "Hello. 911."

____ 2. "This is an emergency!"

____ 3. "Thank you."

____ 4. "My restaurant is across from the laundromat."

B Complete the words in each sentence with one letter. Use the letters in the box.

a	e	i	~~o~~	u

1. I'm g__o__ing t__o__ the b__o__ __o__kst__o__re __o__n the c__o__rner.
2. I go to the p____rk on Mond____ys.
3. Wh____r____ is th____ fir____ station.
4. O____r dr____gstore is next to the co____rtho____se.
5. H____s company ____s buying two apartment bu____ld____ngs on th____s street.

UNIT

12 Yes, I Can!

LESSON 1 VOCABULARY

A Match the words with the pictures.

<u>6</u> secretary	____ painter	____ mechanic
____ cashier	____ housekeeper	____ truck driver
____ salesperson	____ hairdresser	____ gardener

B Look at the pictures in A. Circle *yes* or *no*.

1. Is Alberto a cashier? (yes) no
2. Is Salima a secretary? yes no
3. Is Elena a truck driver? yes no
4. Is Teng a painter? yes no

A **Look at the picture. Complete the sentences. Use the words in the box.**

use computers	sell clothes	cut hair	~~fix cars~~

1. Jim can ___fix cars___.
2. Raja can ______________.
3. Lily can ______________.
4. Leo can ______________.

B **Complete the chart. Use the words in the box.**

~~truck driver~~	gardener	~~drive trucks~~	housekeeper
clean	take care of plants	painter	paint houses

Jobs	Job skills
truck driver	drive trucks

LESSON 3 GRAMMAR

A **Look at the pictures. Complete the sentences. Use *can* or *can't*.**

1. I ____can____ fix cars.
2. I ____________ fix the computer.
3. Dara ____________ fix the computer.
4. Mateo ____________ paint houses.
5. He ____________ speak English.
6. He ____________ drive.

B **Look at the job applications. Write sentences. Use *can* or *can't* and the words in parentheses.**

JOB APPLICATION (142)
Name: Marco Valdez
Current job: salesperson
Job skills:
☑ drive a car
☐ use a computer
☑ speak English
☑ other: sell furniture

JOB APPLICATION (143)
Name: Min Wong
Current job: gardener
Job skills:
☑ drive a car
☐ use a computer
☐ speak English
☑ other: take care of plants

JOB APPLICATION (144)
Name: Alba Montoya
Current job: housekeeper
Job skills:
☐ drive a car
☐ use a computer
☐ speak English
☑ other: clean houses

1. (Marco) ____Marco can sell furniture.____
2. (Marco, Min, and Alba) ____________
3. (Marco and Min) ____________
4. (Min and Alba) ____________
5. (Min) ____________

C Answer the questions. Circle *a* or *b*.

1. Can she cut hair?
   a. Yes, he can. (b.) Yes, she can.
2. Can they write in English?
   a. Yes, we can. b. No, they can't.
3. Can you fix cars?
   a. No, I can't. b. No, you can't.
4. Can he paint a house?
   a. No, he can't. b. No, she can't.
5. Can your brother drive a truck?
   a. Yes, you can. b. Yes, he can.

D Match the questions with the answers.

__d__ 1. Can you use an English dictionary?	a. Yes, they can.
____ 2. Can Mr. Levitt use the Internet?	b. No, he can't.
____ 3. Can Karen drive a truck?	c. No, he isn't.
____ 4. Can they clean houses?	d. Yes, I can.
____ 5. Is he a salesperson?	e. Yes, she can.

E Complete the conversations. Use *can* or *can't*.

1. A: ____Can____ the truck driver fix trucks?
   B: Yes, he ____can____.
2. A: ____________ the cashier fix computers?
   B: No, she ____________.
3. A: ____________ the hairdresser speak English?
   B: Yes, he ____________.
4. A: ____________ the secretary use a computer?
   B: Yes, she ____________.
5. A: ____________ the housekeeper drive?
   B: No, she ____________.

LESSON 4 EVERYDAY CONVERSATION

A **Complete the conversation. Use the words in the box.**

~~truck~~	can't	Yes	evenings

Mrs. Woods: Can you drive a ___truck___$_1$?

Lionel: ________$_2$, I can.

Mrs. Woods: Can you work ________$_3$?

Lionel: No, I ________$_4$.

B **Circle the words that start with *c*.**

A: (Can) you use a (computer?)

B: Yes, I can.

A: Can you sell clothes?

B: No, I can't.

A: Can you drive a car?

B: Yes, I can.

A: Can you clean?

B: Yes, I can.

DO THE MATH Go to page 94.

LESSON 5 READING

A **Read the job ads.**

B **Look at A. Circle *a* or *b*.**

1. work in the evening
   (a.) cashier and dental assistant — b. painter and dental assistant
2. work part time in the morning
   a. painter — b. classroom aide
3. work November and December
   a. classroom aide — b. cashier
4. work full time
   a. painter and dental assistant — b. classroom aide and cashier
5. have a driver's license
   a. cashier — b. painter
6. work on Saturdays
   a. cashier — b. dental assistant

A Complete the sentences. Use the words in the box.

babysitter	painter	can	computers	cashier
truck driver	fix	part time	~~housekeeper~~	

Across

2. A housekeeper can clean.
3. A ________________ can paint houses.
6. Yes, I ________________.
7. A ________________ takes care of children.
8. Melissa is a ________________ at the drugstore.

Down

1. Can you use ________________?
4. A ________________ can drive trucks.
5. Can you work ________________ ?
9. A mechanic can ________________ cars.

B Write the words in the crossword puzzle.

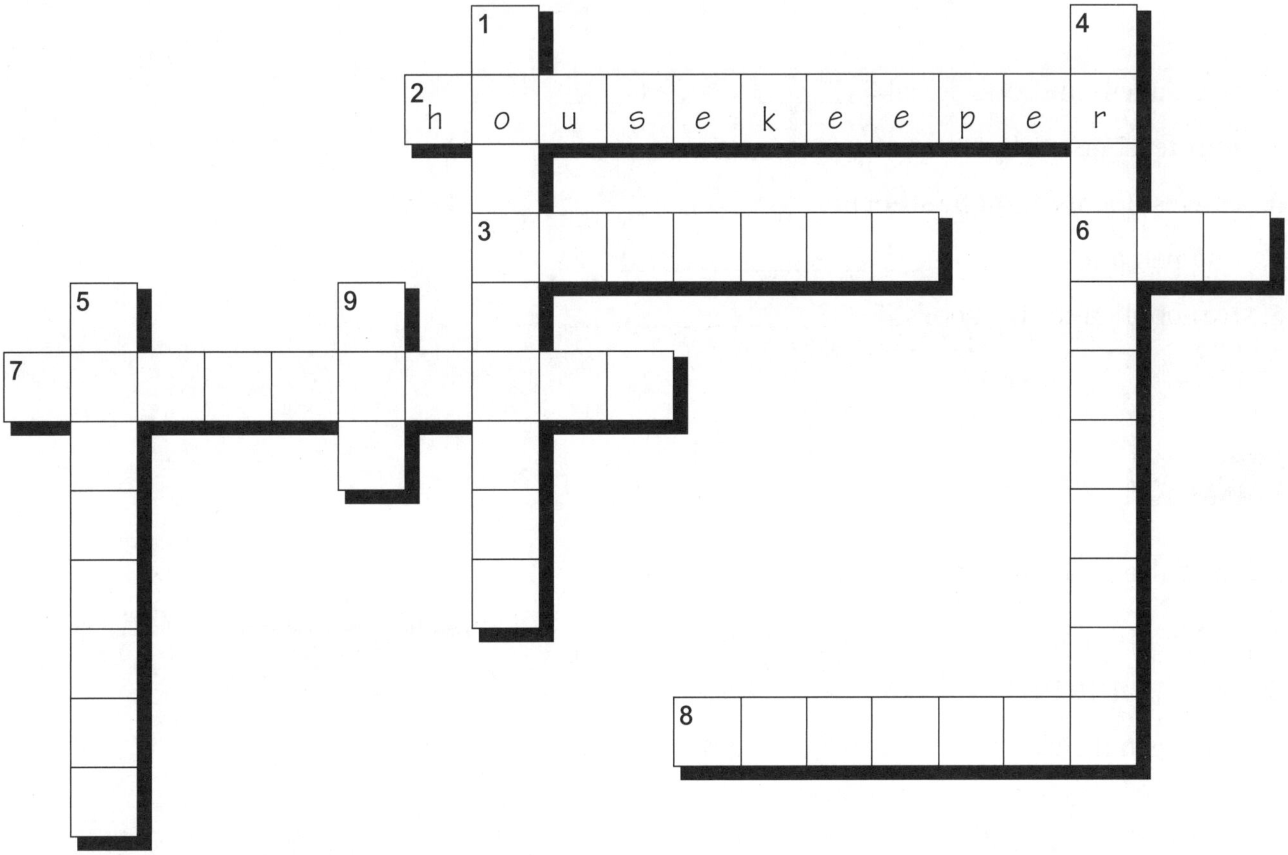

DO THE MATH

UNIT 1

Add the numbers.

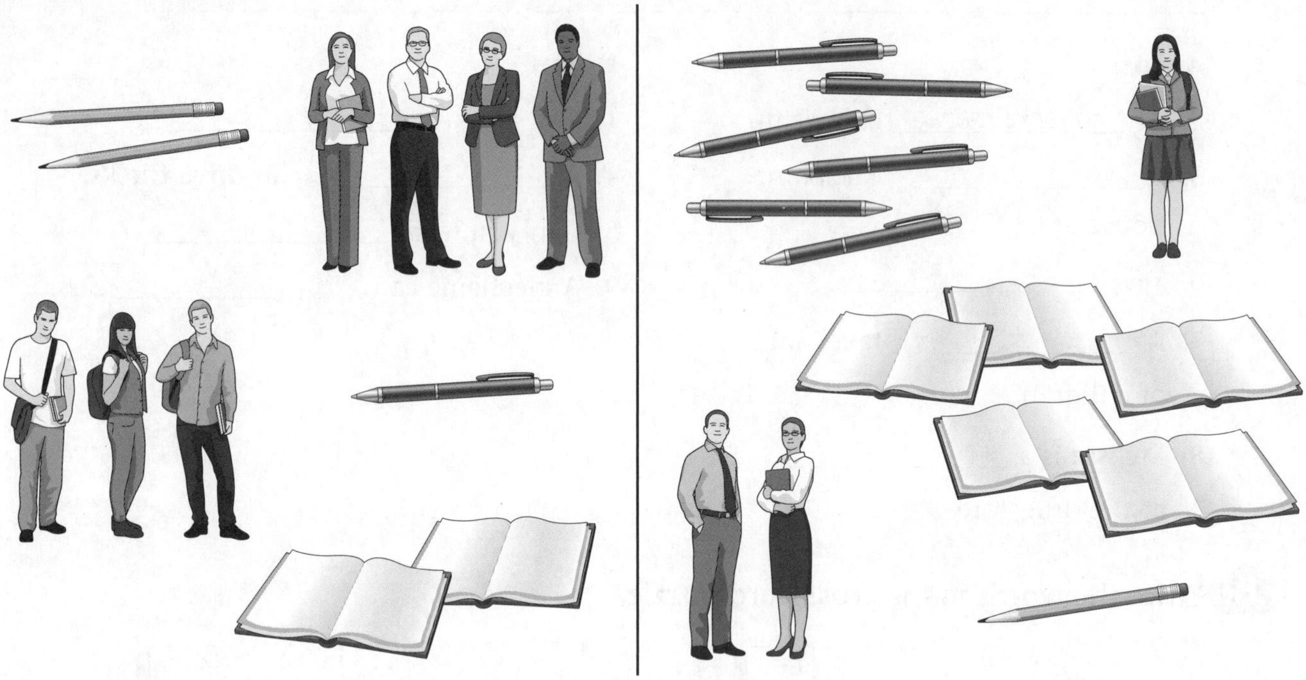

1. two pencils and one pencil = ___3 pencils___
2. four teachers and two teachers = ________________
3. three students and one student = ________________
4. one pen and six pens = ________________
5. two books and five books = ________________

UNIT 2

Look at the picture. Circle *True* or *False*.

1. Kat is sick.	*True* (circled)	*False*
2. Mary is at 102°F.	*True*	*False*
3. Mike is not sick.	*True*	*False*

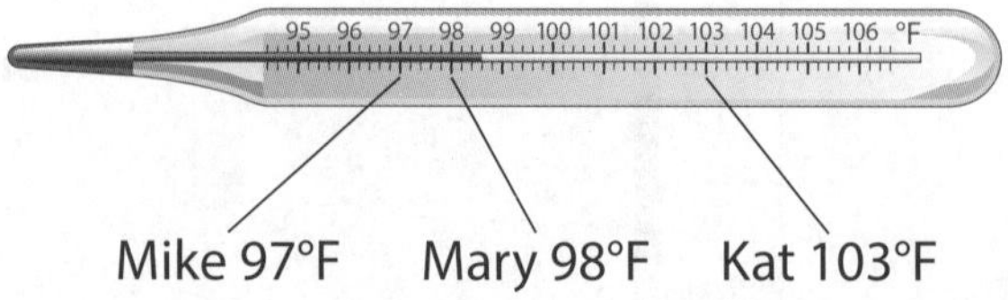

Look at the schedule. Answer the questions. Circle *a* or *b*.

Work Schedule	
Julie	9:00 a.m. - 3: 30 p.m.
Carlos	9:00 a.m. - 5:00 p.m.
Min	11:30 a.m. - 7:00 p.m.
Tom	3: 00 p.m. - 7:00 p.m.

1. How many people are there?
   a. 3 people
   (b.) 4 people
2. How long is Julie working today?
   a. 6 hours and 30 minutes
   b. 5 hours and 30 minutes
3. How long is Carlos working today?
   a. 8 hours
   b. 7 hours
4. How long is Min working today?
   a. 7 hours and 30 minutes
   b. 8 hours and 30 minutes
5. How long is Tom working today?
   a. 5 hours
   b. 4 hours

UNIT 4

Write the correct number.

1. October 3rd – October 10th = ___7___ days
2. February 10th – February 24th = __________ days
3. May 2nd – May 8th = __________ days
4. November 17th – November 28th = __________ days

UNIT 5

Look at the picture. Do the math. Then write the sale price.

1. $8.00 × 0.5 = ___$4.00___ A sweater is ___$4.00___.
2. $25.00 × 0.5 = __________ The pants are __________.
3. $18.50 × 0.5 = __________ The shoes are __________.
4. $12.00 × 0.5 = __________ A shirt is __________.

Do the math and complete the sentence.

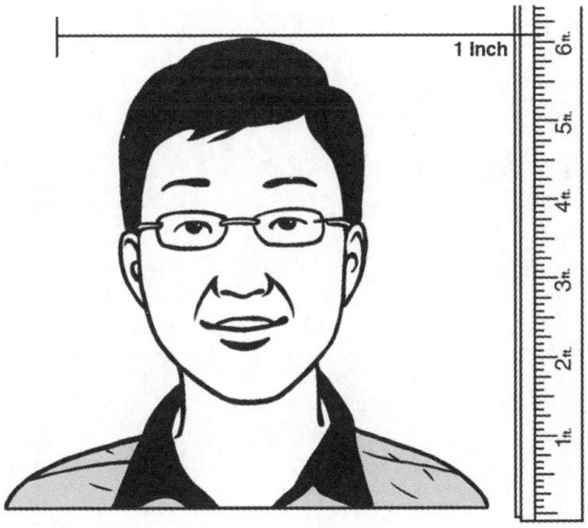

His daughter is three years old.

She is 39 inches tall.

1. His daughter is ____________________ feet and ____________________ inches tall.
2. The father is ____________________ feet and ____________________ inches tall.

Read the problems. Do the math. Write the prices.

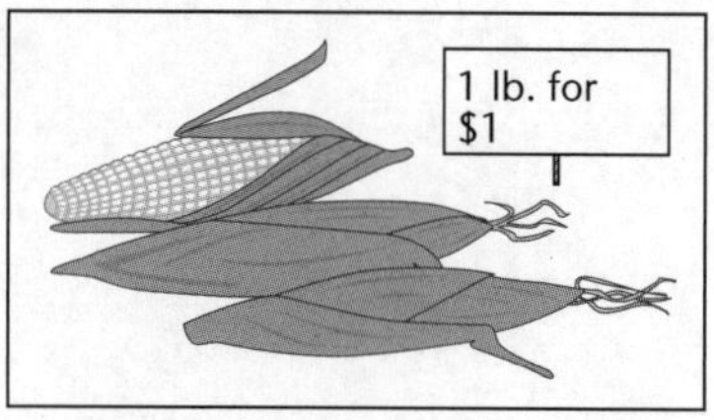

1. We need 3 pounds of corn.

   1 lb × __3__ = 3 lbs.

   $1 × 3 = $ __3__

   3 lbs. of corn = $__3__

2. You need 3 pounds of apples.

   1 lb. × ____ = 3 lbs.

   $2 × 3 = $____

   3 lbs. of apples = $____

3. She needs 4 pounds of broccoli.

   2 lbs. × ____ = 4 lbs.

   $2 × 2 = $____

   4 lbs. of broccoli = $____

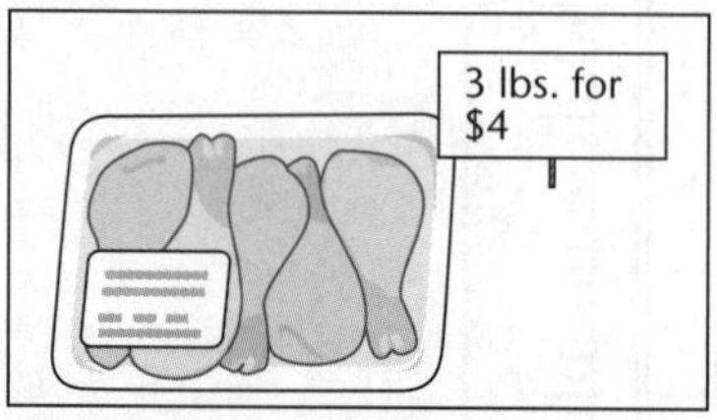

4. I need 6 pounds of chicken.

   3 lbs. × ____ = 6 lbs.

   $4 × 2 = $____

   6 lbs. of chicken = $____

UNIT 8

Look at the pictures. Answer the questions.

1. Take ____ of medicine a day.

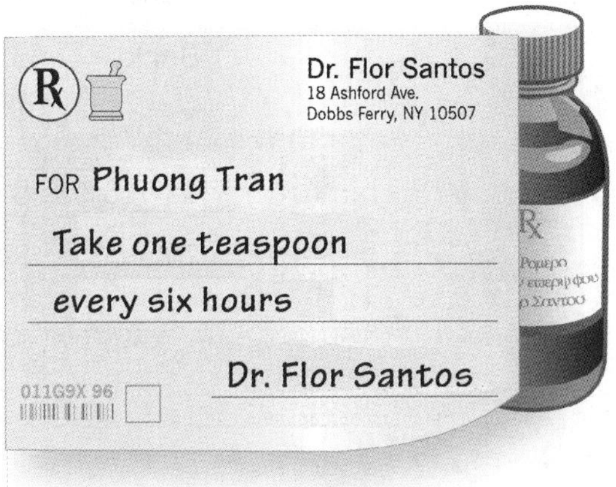

a. 6 teaspoons

b. 4 teaspoons

2. Take ____ of medicine a week.

a. 7 tablespoons

b. 14 tablespoons

3. Take ____ of medicine a day.

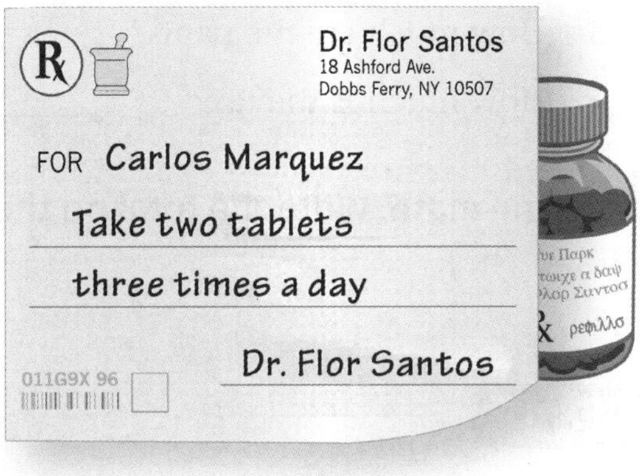

a. 6 tablets

b. 4 tablets

4. Take ____ of medicine a day.

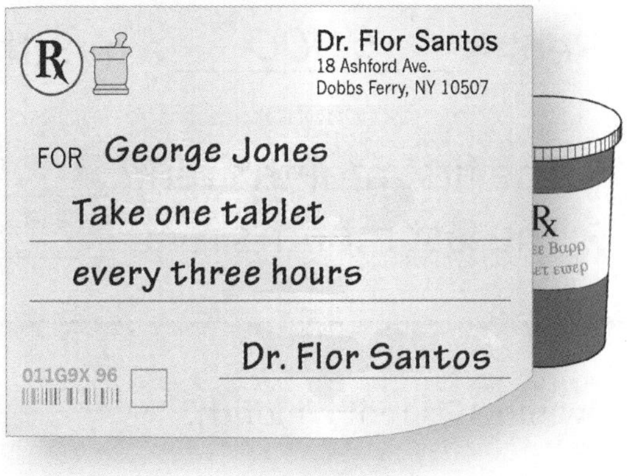

a. 3 tablets

b. 8 tablets

UNIT 9

A **Read the receipt. Answer the questions.**

1. How much are the socks? $3.00
2. How much is the T-shirt? ____________
3. How much are the pants? ____________
4. How much is the tax? ____________

B **Do the math. Write the total on the receipt.**

Clothes Town

08-11-2019 17:12 0196-020 DEP

Pants	$ 35.00
Socks	$ 3.00
T-shirt	$ 12.50
Tax 5%	$ 2.53
Total	$______

CUSTOMER COPY

UNIT 10

Read the information. Do the math. Answer the question.

Green Apartments

Rent is $900 a month. The first month you pay:

- The first month's rent: $900
- The last month's rent: $900

1. How much is rent a month?

   $____________

2. How much do you pay the first month for this apartment?

   $900 + $900 = $____________

UNIT 11

A **Look at the map. Do the math. Complete the sentences.**

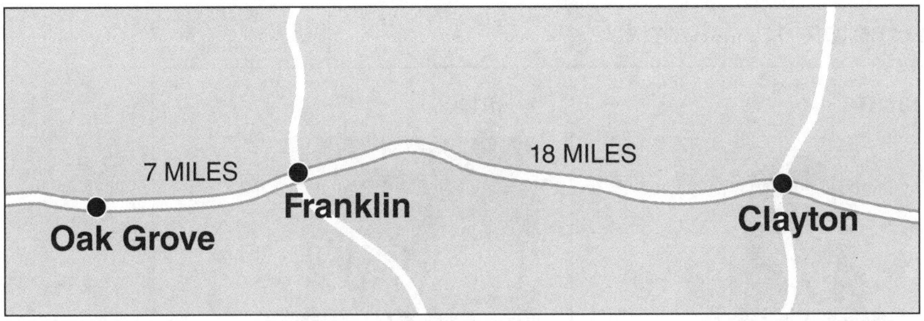

1. Franklin is __7__ miles from Oak Grove.
2. Clayton is ____ miles from Franklin.
3. Clayton is ____ miles from Oak Grove.

B **Look at the map. Do the math. Complete the sentences.**

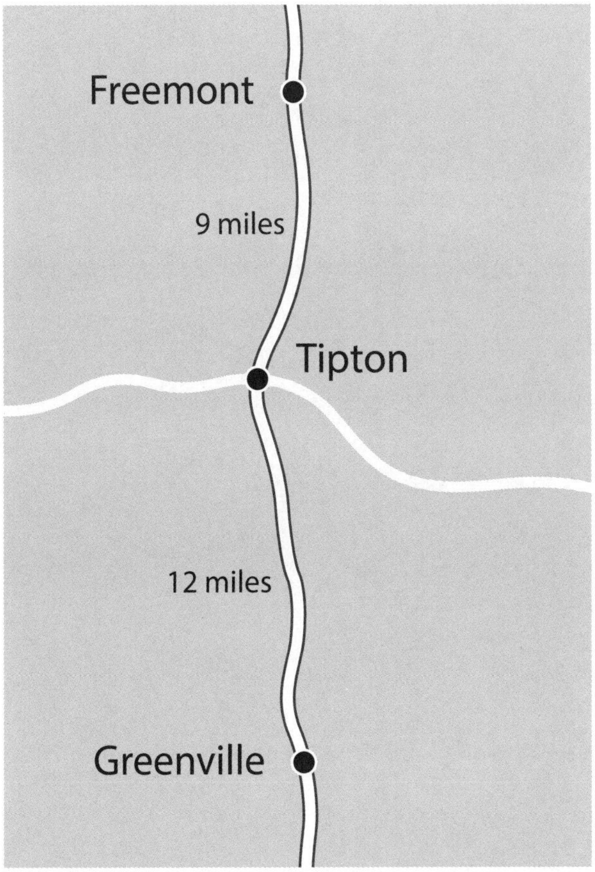

1. Freemont is ____ miles from Tipton.
2. Tipton is ____ miles from Greenville.
3. Freemont is ____ miles from Greenville.

Read the schedule. Do the math.

Work Schedule for Monday		
Juan	Joanna	Charles

8:00 a.m. – 3:00 p.m.	9:00 a.m. – 5:00 p.m.	3:00 p.m. – 9:00 p.m.

1. Juan works ___7___ hours on Monday.
2. Joanna works ____________ hours on Monday.
3. Charles works ____________ hours on Monday.